CHILDHOOD
1892 ~ 1992

Sue C. Wortham

ASSOCIATION FOR
CHILDHOOD EDUCATION INTERNATIONAL
11501 Georgia Avenue, Suite 315, Wheaton, MD 20902
301-942-2443 • 800-423-3563

Cover Design:
Marshal Ross Wortham and
Benjamin Ross Wortham
Desktop Production and Layout:
Benjamin Ross Wortham

Copyright © 1992, Association for Childhood Education International
11501 Georgia Avenue, Suite 315, Wheaton, MD 20902

Library of Congress Cataloging-in-Publication Data
Wortham, Sue Clark, 1935-
    Childhood 1892-1992 / Sue C. Wortham.
      p.   cm.
    Includes bibliographical references.
    ISBN 0-87173-126-6
    1. Early childhood education—United States—History.   I. Title.
LB1139.25.W67   1992
372.21' 0973—dc20   92-27561
                                          CIP

TABLE OF CONTENTS

INTRODUCTION

This publication was written as a celebration; first it celebrates a century of childhood and second, it celebrates the centennial year of the Association for Childhood Education International. Because ACEI has as its major purpose to serve children, it seemed appropriate for this centennial publication to describe childhood and childhood education during the last century–from the last decade of the 19th century to the final decade of the 20th century.

In *A Century of Childhood Education 1892-1992*, the past hundred years have been described in the context of the times and conditions during different periods: prior to 1890, 1890 to 1930, 1930 to 1950, 1950 to 1975 and 1975 to the present. Each period begins with a brief review of major historical events and trends, followed by the types of conditions and lifestyles experienced by diverse populations of children during that segment of history. The history of childhood education for each period includes all levels of education, from the university level to care and learning of very young children. The description of each time period is concluded with a brief history of ACEI as the organization worked within the context of the issues, opportunities and problems of the time.

While this centennial publication focuses on children, a companion centennial publication, *Profiles in Childhood Education 1931-1960*, celebrates the lives and contributions of ACEI leaders. *Profiles* is a sequel to *Dauntless Women in Childhood Education* published in 1972. Through these and other ACEI publications, a comprehensive picture can be drawn of the individual and collective contributions made to children and their education by ACEI through its branches and membership.

I feel most fortunate to have been given the opportunity to develop this special publication. I thank the Executive Board for entrusting the project to me. I also want to acknowledge Stevie Hoffman for her patience and time in making extensive improvements to the original manuscript. Most of all I need to acknowledge Lucy Prete Martin, not only for the support and encouragement she extended in the conceptualization and development of this project, but for her total commitment to all ACEI publications.

Sue C. Wortham
The University of Texas at San Antonio

CHAPTER I
THE AMERICAN EXPERIENCE IN CHILDHOOD AND CHILDHOOD EDUCATION THROUGH THE NINETEENTH CENTURY

The understanding that childhood is a separate period of life is a phenomenon that emerged in the 17th century at the end of the Middle Ages. The American experience of childhood was partially an extension of European influence. American childhood in the 18th and 19th centuries, however, was more than the British and European influence described in so many histories of the country's colonization. Not only were immigrants from other parts of the world involved in the settlement of the colonies and United States, but also natives, both Indian and Hispanic, who had occupied the land for many centuries. Black children born to slaves who were forcibly brought here to help establish the farming industry had a unique type of childhood that was contingent upon the condition of slavery, as well as life as freed people after the Civil War. The history of childhood is their history as well.

In the Middle Ages, individuals were generally ignored until they were no longer children. Babies were separated from their parents and sent out to wet nurses. At the age of 8 or 9, poor children went out into the streets to find work and lodging. Middle–class children also left home for vocational apprenticeship or service. Young children were treated as if they were expendable, partially due to the incredible rate of infant and child mortality. Because of infant and child deaths, parents were hesitant to establish an attachment.

The 17th century saw the evolution of a pattern for the modern family. As lords of manorial communities began divesting large tracts of land, smaller communities began to form. Communal living within the manor was no longer the norm. Families established themselves in their own homes; and as the independence of yeomen and merchants developed, conjugal family life and domestic activities centered around the home. The father assumed responsibilities formerly held by the lord of the manor and the priest. New spiritual reforms encouraged people to learn to read, and privacy and individual freedom led to a new value for individuals and a corresponding interest in childhood (Schorsch, 1979). In the new society of the 17th century, there was an awareness of the particular nature of childhood. Children were given a special costume to separate them from adults. Writers of the period saw children as fragile creatures of God who needed to be safeguarded and reformed (Aries, 1962; Weber, 1984). The 17th century was marked by a new care and concern for childhood that followed immigrants to the new world.

During the Renaissance, several leaders of the time contributed to the understanding of childhood and how children should be reared and educated. The impact of their influence laid the groundwork for efforts on children's behalf that were taken in the 18th and 19th centuries and continue today.

The Renaissance revived an interest in classical learning and religious reformation. Johann Amos Comenius, a Moravian bishop, was a leader in the expansion of educational opportunities through universal education, including children. In *School of Infancy*, Comenius wrote on the training of children under 6 years of age. He outlined a program for young children through play, games, rhymes, fairy tales and manual activity. He expected children to go to school at the age of 6 to receive instruction in the three R's, as well as religion, morals and the mechanical arts.

In France, Jean Jacques Rousseau was more influential than perhaps any other writer of the 18th century. He advocated naturalism and transformed education, particularly for young children, with his view that human nature is essentially good and education must allow that goodness to unfold. In his book *Emile* (1911), Rousseau described what he believed to be the natural characteristics of children at different age levels and outlined the type of education appropriate at each level. For example, he suggested that young children should be free of swaddling and adult clothing and should be allowed to eat, run and play as much as they wanted. He also admonished mothers to trust the child's spontaneous impulses.

Johann Heinrich Pestalozzi translated Rousseau's ideas on education into practice, devoting his life to education of the poor. In schools he developed toward the end of the 18th century, Pestalozzi relied on children's natural instincts to motivate them to learn, using methods that allowed him to adapt instruction to the individual child. He advocated the use of natural objects and self–discovery to teach children through a series of "object lessons" (Weber, 1984).

These three pioneers in the study of childhood, the nature of children and how young children learn not only influenced efforts to improve conditions for children but also influenced childhood education in America. Their ideas were taken by colonists and immigrants to the new world to form the conditions of childhood and education in the 18th and 19th centuries in the United States. As in Europe and other continents, however, the conditions of childhood varied, depending on the education, wealth and opportunities available to the family of the child.

CHILDHOOD IN THE UNITED STATES PRIOR TO 1890

The first immigrants to the continent came from Asia thousands of years ago. They occupied North and South America and were the antecedents of Native American and Hispanic populations living on the continent when settlers began to arrive from Europe. The United States was settled by waves of immigrants from different parts of the world, representing different ethnic groups and cultures, with varied economic, religious and social lifestyles.

Colonization of the east coast began in the 1600s. Many emigrated because of political, religious and economic disruptions in Europe and England. In the early 1600s, 80 percent of the colonial population was English; in the late 1600s and 1700s, immigrants came from northern and western Europe. The Scotch-Irish formed the largest groups, with Germans as the second largest group in the 1700s. Smaller groups of French Huguenots, Welsh, Jews, Swiss and Highland Scots also came during the 1700s (Snapper, 1976).

Black immigrants came as early as the 1600s. The first Black immigrants had legal status. Although both Blacks and Whites owned servants in the early years, Blacks were vulnerable to slavery as the need for labor expanded.

The influx of immigrants between 1850 and 1920 included large numbers of southern and eastern Europeans who suffered from economic and language barriers. These illiterate, semi- and unskilled workers formed an inexpensive labor pool and tended to live in urban slum areas. These laborers were exploited, as were the Black slaves who were freed from slavery at the end of the Civil War.

The abolition of slavery, with a new demand for inexpensive labor, led to an influx of Asian and southern European immigrants. Between the 1850s and 1880s, Chinese immigrants, mostly young males who were characterized as young, thrifty and industrious, settled in western locations of the United States. Japanese also entered the country as family units until the Exclusion Act of 1924 curtailed Asian immigration (Snapper, 1976).

Types of Family Lifestyles
Because the groups that populated the continent were so diverse, there was no

THE MODERN CITY
Hanging on the skirts, very literally of indecision, a small boy wearily trailed his aunt through the splendor of the "ladies' great shop" in New York City in the 1850s. Five stories high, A. T. Stewart's magnificent Marble Palace "bravely waylaid custom" on the Chambers Street corner of Broadway. It regularly interrupted aunt and nephew on their way from a dentist's office on Wall Street, confronting them with displays . . . .

The modern city, providing the economic incentive and the physical setting for new enterprise, produced the department store. The city stimulated the expansion of the retail market, improved communications systems, and generated a new building technology. Swept along by a tide of progress, residents steadily expanded the range of their consumption beyond food and material for clothing; the ambience of the large city encouraged many people of modest affluence to aspire to an air of solid comfort, if not luxury . – Gunther Barth. (1988). The department store. In Timothy J. Crimmins & Neil Larry Shumsky, *American life, American people, Vol. II* p.108. New York: Harcourt Brace Jovanovich.

common family lifestyle. There were some characteristics of living in America, however, that families had in common. From the beginning, all groups were confronted with constant change and challenge. Mobility was a phenomenon of living in America that all early colonists and settlers experienced. This was especially evident during the 1800s when westward expansion, combined with the change from a rural, agrarian society to an urban, industrialized society, had an impact on all populations.

For the most part, family lifestyle was determined by level of education, wealth and status of the family, whether they lived in an urban or rural area and whether they lived in the Northeast, South or western frontier of the continent. Families represented many religions, spoke many different languages and observed a variety of cultural customs. As English gradually became the dominant language, it also became a unifying element in the American experience.

By 1800, eastern urban areas had a three-class society. Wealthy merchant families expanded their business through employment of members of the extended family. Artisans practiced skilled trades and trained apprentices or journeymen to carry on the trade. Laborers, the lowest group, had unstable family and working conditions. The adults died young, their children had little opportunity for training or education and continual poverty was the result (Sudia, 1976).

At the time of the Revolution, families had been in America for 170 years. There were about 3 million people including English, Scots, Irish, Jews, Germans, French, Dutch, Swedes, Africans and Native Americans. Family life and childrearing practices varied widely among social classes and religious groups. Childhood for the child of the wealthy genteel family in the East was different from that of a child in a frontier farm family. Likewise, childhood was different for the child of the southern plantation owner when compared to the Black slave child. Life for a Native American child subjected to wars and frequent relocation contrasted with that of a first generation Italian child living in a tenement in an eastern city.

Religious Beliefs and Childrearing Practices
Family lifestyles and childrearing practices were related to religious beliefs and practices of Protestant Americans in the 17th and 18th centuries. Greven (1977) described these patterns of childrearing in *The Protestant*

Temperament where he discussed three types of family groups: the genteel, the moderate and the evangelical.

The genteel class had fine clothing, libraries, elaborate toys and well-furnished houses. Its members showed concern for the latest fashions and the maintenance of good health. Parenthood was a loving but distant relationship with the children. Children were part of a cohesive and affectionate family, and were indulged by parents, nurses and servants who provided surrogate care.

Moderate families were described as self–controlled and authoritative. Parents set limits and boundaries for their children, and they sought voluntary and affectionate obedience from their children. Children lived with extended families of several generations, with grandparents also exercising authority over the children. The responsibility of the family was to nurture virtue and industry in the children at an early age.

Evangelical parents believed that children were to love and fear both their parents and their God. Evangelical families generally consisted of the immediate family unit, rather than an extended family relationship. The authority of the parents was absolute, while obedience and submission were the only acceptable responses for children. Parents imposed their will upon their infants and small children, which left the children without any rights for their own desires, needs or wishes. Parents believed that their responsibility was to control and break the emerging will of their children during the first years of life.

Evangelical parents were engaged in war with their children, a war which could end only with total victory by the parents and unconditional surrender by the child. The imagery of their warfare is the language of power unchecked and of resistance quelled. Might and right—the prerogatives of parenthood—faced defiance and rebellious willfulness—the characteristics of the unbroken child. Generation after generation of evangelical parents wrote about their battles with pride and contentment that sprang from success. Their children, conquered, submitted and forgot their own early efforts at independence and selfhood. (Greven, 1977, p. 37)

Children of the Poor

Children in the three types of families described by Greven also varied in their wealth and social standing; nevertheless, any suffering they experienced was due to religious factors and preferred styles of living. Children of the poor, in contrast, suffered from the effects of living in poverty.

Poor children might be orphaned, sold by their parents or live in a family unable to support itself. These children—and sometimes entire families—frequently found themselves in almshouses or workhouses as indentured servants, serving an apprenticeship or laboring in a mill or factory.

The early colonists of the 1600s perceived the labor of children as laudable; it prevented them from growing up in idleness. Children were often sent to the colonies in bondage as servants or as apprentices to relieve European and English society from having to support them if they were orphaned or illegitimate.

Colonists also brought the European and English practice of establishing houses of refuge for the handicapped, the insane, the feeble-minded, aged and poor families. In exchange for the opportunity to live in a workhouse or almshouse, the residents repaid their living expenses through labor. This included children, as well as adults. Between 1850 and 1857, reports described miserable conditions in these living quarters. During the following decade and after the end of the Civil War, the number of children in almshouses in New York City increased 300 percent. Abuses in the system, however, turned public opinion against them; and because they were also too costly to operate, they began to be closed in the latter decades of the 19th century (Datta, 1976).

The use of children as servants or apprentices solved community needs for a labor force. For almost 300 years, parents sold their children, or children were taken from families and placed as servants or apprentices or placed in a home to learn a craft or trade. Toward the end of the 18th century, when craft industries began to expand into shops, households included children, servants and apprentices. When further expansion resulted in the establishment of factories, especially textile factories, child labor continued. Between 1790 and 1810, the factory system had spread throughout New England. Although children and women provided 90 percent of the workforce for these factories, entire families often worked in factories and were encouraged to invite their relatives to join them at their place of employment.

During the following century, children of immigrant families poured into the United States. Into the glass factories and mills of the North they went, as children of freed slaves entered the work force of the South. In the coal fields of the Appalachians, children went down into the pits. They rose before dawn, returning after 12 hours of hard, dangerous labor, girls as well as boys. In the factories of the Mid-west the children, their mothers and their fathers rose at 4:30 to the shrilling of the factory whistle and worked, day in and day out, for their mostly short lives. The industrial wealth of the United States was built, according to the records of the 1800s, on the slavery of Blacks and children. (Datta, 1976, p. 267)

The closing of almshouses and workhouses led to the establishment of orphanages in the 19th century. Religious and philanthropic groups started orphanages, soon to be followed by municipal and state orphanages. The quality of care and possible abuse of children became a concern. The move to place children in homes, and the practice of placing children for adoption finally, led to the decline of orphanages.

The large numbers of children of destitute immigrant families living in East Coast cities caused additional problems for these urban areas. Poor children roamed the streets. New York City had about 10,000 vagrant children by 1850, some of whom turned to prostitution and crime to sustain themselves. Many of the children were sent West and South to foster homes. Between 1849 and 1929, the New York Children's Aid Society placed about 100,000 children in foster homes in the South and West. A citizens' committee would arrange for placement of the children with families in their community. Families were not paid to care for the child, but they were able to use the children for farm labor (Datta, 1976).

Toward the end of the 1800s, various types of reforms affecting poor children were making advances. Bondage and apprenticeships had faded away. While child labor was still practiced, children under 16 were protected from its excesses after 1900. The establishment of free public schools resulted in educational opportunities for children working in factories. Child labor laws regulating how many hours children worked plus laws requiring attendance in school gradually contributed to improvements for poor children. The practice of placing poor and orphaned children in the West and South also declined. It was not until well into the 20th century, however, that child labor was eliminated.

Black Children and Native American Children

Black children lived a life of deprivation and cruelty under slavery. Slaves were kidnapped and brought to this continent, usually as individuals. Families established on plantations were frequently torn apart through sales. Parents were separated from one another or their children; siblings were also separated. Children were sent to the fields as young as age 6. They were poorly housed and clothed, and undernourished. As slaves, they had no rights and no education. After slaves were freed, conditions improved only slightly for Black children. Their parents often worked as sharecroppers or tenant farmers for very low wages, and opportunities for education were few for many years. Children were used for child labor in southern industries. It was not until the present century that substantial efforts were made on behalf of Black children and their families.

Life was also extremely difficult for Native American children. The settlement of the East Coast caused Native Americans to be moved west of the Mississippi in the 1830s. Treaties made with Native Americans were violated repeatedly, and their rights were frequently ignored. There were battles and skirmishes between Native Americans and settlers from the first years of colonization until the destruction of Custer's regiment in 1876. In addition, Native Americans were susceptible to European diseases. The death rate from these illnesses was extraordinarily high, coming from epidemics starting in the 1600s and lasting through the 19th century (Snapper, 1976).

Relocation of Native American tribes was frequent. Finally, they were moved to reservations where they were governed and controlled by a paternalistic United States government. The education provided Native American children during the years of colonization and westward expansion came from the tribe. Children were taught the practices, rituals and history of their culture by tribal elders. Literacy as understood by the national American culture became available later when schools were established on reservations and nearby communities.

"Their dear mother was not there"

Health Conditions

Although life experiences for different groups of children varied, one condition was shared by all: the high infant mortality rate. It was not until the last half of the 19th century that people became concerned about the high numbers of deaths in infancy and childhood.

Awareness of the need to know what was causing the deaths and the need for parents to know how to protect the health of their children led to the establishment of organizations concerned with child health. After the Civil War, the city of New York created a Metropolitan Sanitary District and Board of Health. Massachusetts became the first state to have a permanent Board of Health and Vital Statistics. By 1877, 14 states had established state health departments. Foundations and organizations, such as the Russell Sage Foundation, the Commonwealth Fund, the American Medical Association, the American Academy of Pediatrics and the General Federation of Women's Clubs, joined city and state health departments in studying why so many children were dying.

The primary cause of infant deaths was found to be the lack of cleanliness in dairies. A pamphlet published in Rochester, New York, advised mothers to breast feed their babies or give them water during the summer months. Milk stations were established where mothers could obtain clean milk and have their babies weighed. A nurse was available to tell the mother how to provide for her child's health needs (Public Health Service, 1976). Another reason for the high death rate of children was the ignorance of doctors. Dr. Abraham Jacobi, founder of American pediatrics, made the medical profession aware that children were different from adults with different health needs. Dr. Thomas M. Rotch, who first held the chair of pediatrics at Harvard Medical School in 1888, called for a study of the various stages of child development to understand anatomy, physiology and child diseases. The training of doctors, nurses and midwives was expanded to provide better obstetrical care for mothers and newborn babies. As a result of a report on the state of training in the nation's medical schools, many institutions were closed. Others modernized medical education to increase the quality of preparation for doctors, nurses and midwives providing obstetrical and pediatric care.

CHILDHOOD EDUCATION IN THE UNITED STATES PRIOR TO 1890

Education in the colonies and early days of the Republic was patterned on the Old World, just as other values and lifestyles were. Schools had as their purpose educating young people with the knowledge received from England and Europe. With the advent of the American Revolution, these ties were broken and the American form of education gradually emerged.

> Above all, the great spur to learning was the American dream itself. The driving idea was that in this new world a man could fulfill his highest potentialities, become all that he was capable of being. In practice, to be sure, that noble ideal has not been uniformly applied. Throughout our history, considerably less than unlimited individual opportunity has been afforded to various minorities, and perhaps most pervasively to black Americans. The ideal nevertheless persists. (Gross & Gross, 1976, p. 179)

Evolution of Schooling in the New World

In the earliest years of colonization, education was informal and based in the family and community. Children and youth were taught individually in the home through apprenticeships, instruction by parents and community members. Schooling was an integral part of life, although formal education was not the major focus for much of the population (Gross & Gross, 1976).

From the beginning, there was a desire to provide for the education of the elite to lead the masses. The first priority for education in the New World was for higher education. Harvard University was established in 1636, soon followed by William and Mary, Princeton, Pennsylvania, Rutgers, Dartmouth and King's College which later became Columbia University (Snyder, 1972). These early institutions, and the 264 others that were established by 1856 in the continental United States, followed a classical curriculum dominated by Latin and Greek. The need to prepare students for college admission led to the establishment of Latin Grammar Schools at the secondary level. All of these institutions enrolled only White men.

Before and after the Revolutionary War, with westward expansion and the industrial revolution, it became apparent that secondary education programs beyond Latin Grammar Schools were needed to provide education and training in mathematics, surveying, bookkeeping and navigation. Benjamin Franklin founded the Franklin Academy in 1751 to meet this need. Many other vocational training academies soon followed. They gradually included some of the classic curriculum along with vocational training.

THE AMERICAN SUNDAY SCHOOL UNION
The American Sunday School Union was one of the philanthropic organizations that conducted schools for children of the poor, particularly children who labored in mills and factories. As the frontier moved West, Sunday Schools were frequently the first school to be established in a community before the community itself could provide for schooling. Although the schooling materials had as their purpose to teach basic literacy, they frequently included moral and religious topics. Lynn, R. W., & Wright, E. (1971). *The big little school*. New York: Harper & Row.

Schooling for Younger Children

Although the government of Massachusetts Bay enacted the first statute to establish a system of schools in 1647, the law was poorly enforced (Snyder, 1972). Nevertheless, the statute set an example for a system of schooling that later led to the establishment of free public education (Gulliford, 1984).

The 1647 law specified that petty schools be established so that children and apprentices could learn to read and write. Selectmen in townships were to provide for the schools, while parents in the district were to construct the school buildings. Where the schools were actually constructed, school was only held for a few months a year when children could be released from the demands of the farm (Snyder, 1972).

As the population increased in the colonies, more well-to-do parents utilized another type of education, subscription schools, to educate their children. Schools were financed by subscriptions, tuition, land rental fees and taxes. White middle-class and upper-class children stayed in school longer and learned business and academic skills (Gulliford, 1984).

Less affluent families collectively employed a mother, widow or unmarried female to teach a group of children in home settings called Dame Schools. Children were taught to read, write and recite scriptures from the Bible. Girls also learned household skills, while boys learned to help around the farm to prepare them for later apprenticeships. The primary curriculum in all colonial schools was scripture, biblical teachings and in some, Latin. Reading, writing and arithmetic were of secondary importance.

Schooling After the American Revolution

Up until the Revolution, schooling for young and older students followed that of England and Europe. Parents wanted their children to retain the religious and secular culture brought across the Atlantic. They feared that future generations would lose their religious values and grow up in ignorance (Handlin, 1976). With the advent of hostilities leading to the Revolutionary War, books and curriculum materials from England were no longer available and were considered unsuitable. American leaders, caught up in the new nationalism, began massive efforts to produce American publications. While Noah Webster compiled spellers and dictionaries to reflect American English, English textbooks were revised, including the *New England Primer* (Bonn, 1976; Handlin, 1976).

The establishment of the new republic and the expansion of the country across the continent, combined with the change from an agrarian economy to an industrial nation, were reflected in expansion and changes in education. The Civil War and its aftermath added the difficulties of a divided nation to the growth process of the educational system. The war was devastating to the people and the economy; however, the continuing development of the nation resulted in new opportunities and complexities for chidren's education after 1850.

Efforts to Establish Public Schools

The American ideal of providing a free public education for all of its citizens was difficult to achieve. Only through publicly funded education could all children have an opportunity for literacy. Such efforts began in the Midwest, but with higher education. In 1830, Oberlin College was founded, the first institution to admit women and Blacks. In the 1850s, Antioch College and state universities in Utah, Michigan, Ohio and Wisconsin became coeducational.

The process of providing equal educational opportunities at the secondary and elementary levels moved much more slowly. The industrial revolution brought large numbers of immigrants from abroad and found American families migrating to urban areas in search of employment. The result was crowded living conditions in the cities. Living circumstances in the tenements aroused public awareness to the plight of children and their need for an education; nevertheless, and at first, it was left to philanthropic resources such as The Society for the Education of the Male Poor and The Society for the Education of the Female Poor to finance schools for poor children (Snyder, 1972).

Frontier and Rural Schools

As the migration of families moved West and South, seeking to escape urban crowding and find new economic opportunities, frontier schools became necessary for the children. While the Northwest Ordinances of 1784, 1785 and 1787 allowed public lands to be leased to benefit public schools, the abundance of free land precluded that method of funding schools. The only reliable source for funding frontier and rural schools was the parents. One-room schools began to dot the frontier as families in a community constructed a building and hired a teacher to instruct their children. School terms and teachers' salaries varied according to the wealth and stability of the families supporting each school (Gulliford, 1984). The schools were frequently overcrowded, and teaching materials meager.

The struggle for publicly funded education gathered strength after the Civil

MASON STREET SCHOOL

The Mason Street school was the first schoolhouse built in San Diego, California in 1865. The first teacher of the school was Mary Chase Walker from Massachusetts. She described her arrival in San Diego and her early experiences at the school:

I arrived in the bay of San Diego on the morning of July 5, 1865. It was a most desolate looking landscape. The hills were brown and barren; not a tree or green thing was to be seen. Of all the dilapidated, miserable looking places I had ever seen this was the worst. The buildings were nearly all of adobe, one story in height, with no chimneys. Some of the roofs were covered with tile and some with earth. The first night of my stay at the hotel a donkey came under my window and saluted me with an unearthly bray. The fleas were plentiful and hungry. Mosquitoes were also in attendance. An Indian man did the cooking and an Irish boy waited on me at the table, and also gave me the news of the town. The landlord told me I could go into the kitchen and cook whatever I wanted if I didn't like the Indian's style and I availed myself of this privilege. I rented two rooms in the Robinson house for $2 a month. My school was composed mostly of Spanish and half-breed children, with a few English and several Americans. I aimed to teach what would be most meaningful to them; namely, reading, spelling, arithmetic, and how to write letters. At recess the Spanish girls smoked cigaritas and the boys amused themselves by lassoing pigs, hens, etc. The Spanish children were very irregular in their attendance at school on account of so many fiestas and amusements of various kinds. For a week before a bull-fight the boys were more or less absent, watching preparations, such as fencing up the streets leading to the plaza.– From leaflet, Mason St. School, San Diego County Historical Days Association.

War. Important educators such as Horace Mann, Samuel Lewis and Henry Barnard came to view education as a public responsibility. At the same time, Emma Willard, Catherine Beecher and Mary Lyon tried to convince women that they should become teachers. The concept of a free public education was established by 1860, but full implementation in practice took many years to accomplish.

Children of all ages attended school together in rural one-room schoolhouses. They frequently entered school as young as 3 or 4 to be watched over by their older brothers and sisters. Boys of 17 and 18 attended during the winter months when the weather prohibited farm work. Farmhands and adult immigrants might also attend during the cold weather (Gulliford, 1984).

Students in these one-room schools were not organized by age or grade, but by ability. Although teachers prepared lessons to match the progress and ability of individual children, many assignments were similar for a group of students. Younger students heard lessons over and over as different groups read or recited for the teacher. Older students not only helped younger children with their lessons, but assisted with classroom duties such as feeding wood to the heating stove, bringing in water and warming lunches. Discipline was very strict and teachers demanded obedience from the children.

Classroom conditions, too, were a factor in the education process. Teachers and students were forced to endure cramped classrooms and overcrowding. In winter there were additional hardships. The smells of wet wool clothes and bags of asafetida, an offensive-smelling resinous material hung around children's necks as health amulets, drove many teachers to open the windows, only to be met with a blast of icy wind. As soon as the window was closed, the air again became stuffy. Students alternately froze and roasted, depending on their proximity to the potbellied stove. The corners of the room could be almost as cold as the out-of-doors. The constant freezing and thawing of the children's feet often gave them chilblains, which made their feet itch intensely as they warmed up, so that throughout the day the room resounded with the constant noise of boots shuffling under desks. (Gulliford, 1984, p. 48)

The important curriculum components were reading, grammar and spelling.

The primer had all three components combined in one textbook. Children were expected to master reading to *McGuffey's Third Eclectic Reader*. After the 1870s, a system of eight grade levels was instituted as education standards were raised. Grammar was taught through exercises in diagramming or parsing, while spelling included recitations and monthly spelldowns with rival districts (Gulliford, 1984). Only cursive writing was taught in the early years. Teachers were required to drill the students in writing skills until their penmanship became neat and legible.

Schooling for Black Children

Contrary to common understanding, education was available for some Blacks in New England colonies early in the nation's history. Slaves were taught so that they could read the Bible and lead useful lives. The schools were funded through philanthropic efforts and contributions made by free Blacks, Black churches and fraternal societies. Although inferior to those in the North, there were also schools in the South for Black children prior to the Revolutionary War (Farmer, 1976). After the war, however, the teaching of Blacks was forbidden by law with harsh penalties resulting for disregarding that law. Schools were disbanded, but hidden efforts for education continued until the end of the Civil War.

After the Civil War, one reconstruction effort was to establish schools for Blacks. Northern teachers, Black churches and fraternal organizations worked with local Black citizens to educate Black people. The Freedman's Bureau under the War Department developed a partnership with the other organizations and aid societies to build over 4,000 schools. Howard University in Washington, D.C., along with other institutions for higher education such as Atlanta University, Fisk, Talladega, Tougaloo and Hampton, were established with assistance from the Freedman's Bureau. Despite these efforts, education for Blacks was inferior or lower in quality than schools for Whites.

The Freedman's Bureau was dismantled in 1875 after only five years of work. Blacks were then forced to form schools as best they could with few resources. Rural schools for Blacks were crude, often abandoned structures that had been used for livestock. Northern philanthropists assisted in improving these schools with funds for both building schoolhouses and purchasing books.

THE OLD COUNTRY SCHOOL
When the county superintendents began their work in the Civil War period, no Midwestern country school was graded. The teachers, still teaching as they had been taught, organized their schools around a series of readers, usually McGuffey's or copies of McGuffey's. Usually there were six readers in the series, each corresponding very loosely to a grade, so that a student in the first reader might be thought to be in the first grade.

From the first reader the teacher taught her students how to read. From those following, particularly the fourth, fifth, and sixth, she taught history from historical accounts and speeches of great men, and elocution and literature from the very best in the English language. Besides the readers, the teacher taught arithmetic, usually from Ray's *New Arithmetic* series and geography from James Monteith's *National Geographical* series.

In the nineteenth century no one really dignified this system by naming it, but modern educators might have called it "self-paced." Students read through the readers at their own pace, and along the way picked up as much arithmetic, geography, and grammar as the teacher could find time to give them. When they had read through the sixth reader they had gone as far as they could go, at least in reading. Many students never made it that far, and years later they would tell their children or grandchildren that they had gone through the third or fourth reader in school, which would completely mystify a generation grown accustomed to the graded school. – Wayne E. Fuller. (1982). *The old country school* (pp. 147-148). Chicago: The University of Chicago Press.

There was also a shortage of Black teachers in the rural South; many educated Blacks migrated to the West and to cities where there was more opportunity. The attitudes of southern Whites against the Black schools caused hardships. Northern teachers who went South to educate Blacks were frequently denied room and board. School buildings were burned, stoned and even shot at by Whites (Gulliford, 1984).

Schooling for Native American Children

Schooling for Native Americans was under the jurisdiction of the United States government. By the end of the 19th century, a system of boarding schools was established away from the reservations. Students were not permitted to wear their native clothing; boys' hair was cut short; and efforts were made to educate students away from their Indian culture, values and customs.

There were also one-room schoolhouses on the reservations established by missionaries. These became day schools that were controlled by the Bureau of Indian Affairs. Thus education for Native Americans, like education for Blacks, was segregated and of a lower quality than that for Whites (Farmer, 1976).

How, then, does one characterize the system of American education prior to 1890? Patricia Graham described it as follows:

Thus, not until the latter part of the 19th century could the United States really be said to have an "educational system" as such, because until that time education had been acquired through a variety of rather haphazard methods. Children studied at home with their parents or with a tutor, or perhaps at the home of a nearby spinster or widow in a "Dame school" with a few neighborhood children, and only rarely at a building formally designated "school" and subsidized by the local community, the church, the children's tuition, private beneficence, or some combination of these. Such formal work often was supplemented by individual study, by perusal of books and local newspapers and journals, by instructional messages embedded in sermons and Sunday School programs, and through apprenticeships both formal and informal to persons who had achieved some degree of mastery of a particular field. (Graham, 1976, p. 135)

ROOTS OF EARLY CHILDHOOD EDUCATION AND CARE PRIOR TO 1890

The years after the end of the Civil War to the turn of the century were a period of establishment and expansion of public school systems throughout the continental United States. They were also a time when attention was focused on preschool children and the need to improve conditions for children of the poor, particularly in urban ghettos and tenements. The advent of the kindergarten, imported from Germany, served as the vehicle whereby philanthropic efforts could be made to assist and educate the poor by serving the needs of young children and their families.

By 1855, the Puritan belief in original sin and children as innately depraved was giving way to ideas based on Romanticism and Rousseau's assertion of the natural goodness of man. The American democratic view also facilitated this change in attitude about the nature of children. The notion that the child is born with inherent impulses that are right and good allowed an understanding of Rousseau's advocacy of a return to nature; that education must allow the goodness in the child to unfold (Weber, 1969; Weber, 1984). The acceptance of play as a medium for educational experience fit within this new perspective of the child.

Friedrich Froebel had also developed his philosophy of the education of young children based on Rousseau's naturalism and Pestalozzi's ideas of education. He applied this philosophy in the development of the first kindergarten in Germany in 1837. Froebel embraced the active nature of learning and saw play as the educational method whereby the child's inner powers could be released. His preschool curriculum focused on the developmental needs of young children and

FIRST FREE KINDERGARTEN WEST OF THE ROCKIES
Of the forty who were accepted the first morning, thirty appeared to be either indifferent or willing victims, while ten were quite the reverse. These screamed if the maternal hand were withdrawn, bawled if their hats were taken away, and bellowed if they were asked to sit down. This rebellion led to their being removed to the hall by their mothers, who spanked them vigorously every few minutes and returned them to me each time in a more unconquered state, with their lung power quite unimpaired and views of the New Education still vague and distorted. As the mothers were uniformly ladies with ruffled hair, snapping eyes, high color and short temper, I could not understand the children's fear of me, a mild young thing . . . but they evidently preferred the ills they knew. When the last mother led in the last freshly spanked child and said as she prepared to leave: "Well I suppose they might as well get used to you one time as another, so good-day, Miss, and God help you!" I felt that my woes were greater than I could bear, for, as the door closed, several infants who had been quite calm began to howl in sympathy with their suffering brethren. – Kate Wiggin. (1925). The girl and the kingdom (pp. 14-15). ACEI Archives.

THE CINCINNATI KINDERGARTEN TRAINING SCHOOL
Adeline S. Kraft was a student at Cincinnati Kindergarten Training School headed by Annie Laws. She later recalled her experiences in a letter to Mary Leeper, Executive Secretary of ACE in 1941. Annie Laws was president of the International Kindergarten Union in 1904 and 1905. Adeline Kraft described one experience as follows:
Another time, Miss Laws was late coming to breakfast–some of us knew why–others didn't. There was an old-fashioned grate in the bedroom Miss Laws occupied (We called it the "Royal Suite."). While Miss Laws was in the shower-room, we hid some of her necessary garments in the grate. It was the custom for all of us to stand behind our chairs in the dining-room, until all the guests were there–so we stood and waited, and waited, and waited. Finally, in Miss Laws came, completely dressed and at ease, her own serene self with a good morning smile for all of us. Those of us who had perpetrated the "crime" felt like crawling under the table. Again, she made no mention of her misplaced belongings, but we are still wondering how she found them, as they had been carefully wrapped in newspapers, tied with string, placed in the grate and lumps of coal put on top—to look like the paper and coal were all ready to burn when a fire was needed. – Letter from Adeline Kraft to Mary Leeper, 1941, ACEI Archives Record Group 1, Box 1.

within a framework of "gifts and occupations," songs, games and movement plays.

In 1856, one of Froebel's students, Margarethe Schurz who had been trained in his methods, opened the first American kindergarten in Watertown, Wisconsin. Although this and other early kindergartens were taught in German to serve the children of German immigrants, the concept of such a program was introduced at a time in American history when there was a need and interest in programs for children too young to attend public schools.

Between 1880 and 1900, more than 10 million immigrants arrived in the United States. These impoverished families did not assimilate quickly into American society as earlier immigrants had. They were frequently illiterate with few employment skills. They tended to stay in urban ghetto tenements. Because both parents worked long hours at poorly paid jobs, the youngest children were often unsupervised for most of the day. Middle-class women, who were members of rapidly expanding women's clubs, philanthropic societies and religious groups, discovered the kindergarten movement to be the answer to their quest for providing care and education for these urban immigrant children (Hewes, 1986).

Most of the first kindergartens were private, such as the one established by Margarethe Schurz in her home. Elizabeth Peabody and her sister, Mary Mann, along with Henry Barnard and William T. Harris, were some of the leaders in advocating for kindergartens. Various philanthropic individuals and organizations began to develop kindergartens in order to render social services that would alleviate conditions for young children living in the slums. The Women's Christian Temperance Union established kindergartens in at least 20 large cities. Mrs. Pauline Agassiz Shaw established 31 free kindergartens in the Boston area by 1883.

Training schools were established to meet the growing need for trained kindergarten teachers. John Kraus and his wife, Maria Kraus, conducted the New York Seminary for kindergarten teachers in New York City. Elizabeth Peabody spent several years training teachers, as did Susan Blow and others.

The kindergarten movement soon became part of public schools. In 1873, William T. Harris and Susan Blow incorporated the first kindergarten program into a public school system in St. Louis. Other school systems also began to support the kindergarten movement and introduced kindergartens into their elementary schools (Weber, 1969).

The growth of the kindergarten movement was rapid. Weber reported that, in 1870, there were fewer than 12 kindergartens in the United States, but by 1880 there were almost 400 kindergartens in 30 states. Many of the kindergarten programs begun as philanthropic efforts were later absorbed into public school systems. In 1872, William T. Hailmann presented Froebelian principles to a general session of the National Education Association. A Department of Kindergarten Instruction was established within NEA in 1885 to explain and promote Froebelian principles, discuss training of kindergarten teachers and advocate kindergartens for all children (Weber, 1969).

By 1890, charity kindergartens began to decline; 10 years later, they had almost disappeared. Public school kindergartens had continued to expand, but there was conflict developing over the direction of the programs in public schools. The naturalism promoted in the original Froebelian kindergarten was being transformed as kindergarten teachers were pressed to conform to the educational demands of the upper grades (Hewes, 1985). Anna E. Bryan first discussed the problems of formalizing kindergartens in a meeting of the kindergarten department of the National Education Association in 1890. Many educators were seeking new procedures for teaching, while others, such as Susan Blow, were rigidly adhering to original Froebelian methods and were unwilling to deviate from traditional procedures (Weber 1969).

When, at a meeting of the National Education Association in1892, a small group of kindergarten educators led by Sarah H. Stewart met in Saratoga Springs, New York, to organize their own advocacy group, massive changes in early childhood education had just begun. The struggles to improve kindergarten programs and the impact of the field of psychology and scientific thinking were yet to gain momentum. The young organization, to be called the International Kindergarten Union, would have a dramatic and sometimes heated role in the evolution of the educational, economic and social changes that were to affect children in the 20th century (Smith, 1942).

CHAPTER 2
EXPANSION AND CHANGE IN CHILDHOOD AND CHILDHOOD EDUCATION: 1890 – 1930

By the last decade of the 19th century, the United States was quite developed compared to its status in 1800. The population had doubled between 1860 and 1900, from 31,000,000 to 76,000,000. Thanks to the five continental railroads connecting East to West and North to South, most of the continental United States had been settled, although some western areas were sparsely populated (Snyder, 1972).

Mechanization and inventions had changed the nation into a strong agricultural and industrial economy that encouraged rural and western settlement. Inventions such as the reaper, thresher, telephone, telegraph and electricity made possible more efficient use of time and resources. Small companies and individual artisans declined as large, nationally run corporations replaced them.

Agricultural and industrial development resulted in the accumulation of vast fortunes for a few in all sections of the United States. Even more important was the rise of the increasingly powerful business class that not only controlled corporations, but also sought to assert its leadership in American politics and society (Henretta, Brownlee, Brody & Ware, 1987). The aristocracy of prosperity was not shared by all, particularly the laborers or working class. The American Federation of Labor, established and led by Samuel Gompers, advocated for the rights and needs of workers. Under the leadership of the AFL, trade unions organized collectively to protect their interests (Beard & Beard, 1944).

Industrialization also led to urbanization. Large cities, such as Cleveland, Pittsburgh and Birmingham, grew rapidly as industrial corporations expanded. Urban growth created a society divided by class, with the poor laborers concentrated in the factory districts, the rising middle class in the suburbs and the wealthy on country estates or in exclusive urban neighborhoods.

Immigration continued to contribute to population growth between 1890 and 1930. The largest numbers came from southern Italy, with smaller groups entering from Austria-Hungary, Poland and Russia (Snyder, 1972; Sudia, 1976). At the same time, infant mortality rates

Syrian Children at Mayer Chapel Kindergarten, 1910

THE TELEPHONE
The telephone came to America—and to the rest of the world—on March 10, 1876; on that day, as far as is known, Alexander Graham Bell became the first person to transmit speech electrically. The American response to that event included a mixture of wonder, confusion, and sheer disbelief. That spoken words could be converted into electrical waves, transmitted along wire, and then reconverted into sound at the other end of the line could not easily be comprehended even after the telephone had been widely described. Perhaps the best way to understand one of Graham Bell's incredulous contemporaries is to imagine how we would feel if we were told that a way had been devised to make extrasensory perception a means of communication. – Sidney A. Aronson. (1977). *Bell's electrical toy: What's the use?* In I. deSola Pool (Ed.), *The social impact of the telephone.* Cambridge: MIT Press.

---

were dropping and life expectancy extended for all populations. Efforts to improve health conditions, particularly for infants and children, strongly contributed to the decline in early deaths by 1930.

Although strides had been made in the establishment of public schools, illiteracy rates were still high, particularly among non-Whites and immigrants. Newer immigrants tended to cluster in urban areas, unlike earlier waves of settlers who followed population trends to western sections of the country. The overpopulation in urban tenements and poor living conditions in industrial areas compounded the health and economic problems of these later immigrants.

Efforts to improve living conditions and educational opportunities for children were steadily progressing, although not all children benefitted equally. Events such as the first of a series of White House Conferences on Children and Youth in 1909, however, heralded a new era in sensitivity to the problems and needs of poorer children and measures to improve conditions for all children. An outcome of the conference was the establishment of the Children's Bureau that worked to outlaw child labor and encouraged the passage of compulsory school attendance laws (Heath, 1976).

CHILDHOOD IN THE UNITED STATES: 1890-1930
While westward settlement marked much of the 19th century, this expansion was largely completed by 1890. The trend from a rural agricultural society to an urban industrial one began before 1890 and continued into the 20th century. Family mobility continued to be an American phenomenon; but the movement now was to the cities where work was to be found in factories, rather than on rural farms. Accordingly, the growth and expansion of large cities predominated during this period. The needs of children, particularly those residing in urban areas, stimulated efforts to improve opportunities and services that would result in better education and quality of life.

The experience of childhood was changing at the turn of the century. In earlier historical periods, survival of the family was the main goal. Children worked to help keep the family fed and clothed, and religious and economic factors dictated that children had little time to be idle. Now, the prosperity of a nation that was settled and established with a growing industrial economy, along with the expansion of educational opportunities for both males and females, resulted in fewer children working and more time spent in school. With the evolution of universal education and laws requiring attendance, children spent many hours each day in school, but also had time for recreation and play. Whereas the family had been the predominant influence on the child's development, other influences, including the school and social settings, now affected the child's values and attitudes.

Industrialization, urbanization and expansion of schooling led to concern for how children and youth spent their leisure time. Various organizations established programs for children and youth, especially for those crowded into slum or industrial areas (Reynolds, 1976). Many of these efforts were geared for older children working in industrial occupations, but opportunities for school children and very young children were also included in programs developed by voluntary and philanthropic organizations.

Settlement houses, established to help poor families living in urban slums, also addressed recreational needs of children. These social centers in crowded neighborhoods provided space for activities and offered services such as homes for working girls and boys, clubs for boys and for girls, music instruction, arts and crafts workshops and playgrounds.

Voluntary organizations concerned for the play and leisure time of children and youth were organized. The YWCA, organized in 1874, and the YMCA, in 1885, provided physical, social and cultural activities for young working men and women. Other voluntary youth organizations had similar goals for children and youth: Boys Club of America (1906), Campfire Girls (1910), Girl Scouts (1912) and Boy Scouts (1929) (Reynolds, 1976).

The playground and recreation movement resulted from the interest in providing safe places for urban children to play and for working youth to spend their recreational time. The early founders of the movement were concerned that older children have opportunities for wholesome recreation, partly to prevent juvenile delinquency. They were also interested in establishing play areas for young children during the summer months and facilitating activities for school-age children throughout the year.

The first playground, the Boston Sand Garden, was developed in 1885 when several large sand piles were placed at the Children's Mission on Parmeter Street. Other playgrounds soon followed in Massachusetts and other states. In 1906, the

---

CONEY ISLAND

People probably enjoyed Coney for a number of reasons. First, the experience of the rides and the bustling midway was structured, fast-paced and extroverted. It allowed ordinary people to leave their cares momentarily behind and to escape into a fantasy land. Second, the atmosphere was sensuous and sensual. The crowds, the bands, the lights, the food and drink were seductive in themselves; but the rides and amusements also offered the promise of sanitized sex. Air jets in the funhouses lifted girls' skirts, couples were squeezed together by the force of the rides, and the promise of the sign by the roller coaster that, "she will throw her arms around your neck," was not lost on the crowd.

Third, the increasing pace and increasing mechanization of life may have made solitude and introspection unwelcome strangers to workers and business people alike. Mechanized, time structured leisure may simply reflect mechanized time structured lives. Fourth and finally, Coney's technological wonders allowed people to participate vicariously in the myth of progress, and to use technology for escape—as a contrast to their common experience of growing constraints and frustrations imposed upon daily life by the engine of technical change. – Robert E. Snow & David E. Wright (1976). Coney Island: A case study in popular culture and technical change. *Journal of Popular Culture, 9,* 960-964.

Playground Association of America was organized in Washington, D.C.; and, by 1910, manufacturers' catalogs featured iron, steel and wooden equipment for playgrounds (Frost & Wortham, 1988).

The Middle-Class Child: Play and Toys

The new, salaried middle-class family brought a new emphasis on family life. These urban middle–class families preferred to live outside the city in the suburbs. The advent of the streetcar and other forms of motorized transportation enabled the father, generally the major support of the family, to travel back and forth to his place of employment. The mother's place was at home with the children. Her responsibility was to manage the activities of the home and nurture the family.

Middle-class children no longer were working members of the family; their responsibility within an extended childhood was to complete a formal education and prepare for adulthood. Leisure time became an important part of childhood. Family excursions to the beach, amusement parks, or public playgrounds and sports activities were engaged in by the entire family. Baseball games were a popular summertime pastime. Families also went to public libraries and attended cultural events. Their children used leisure time after school and on weekends and holidays for play. The comfortable financial status of the family made it possible for parents to provide their children with toys for play.

Toys had been available for centuries. In medieval times, hoops, hobbyhorses and other toys frequently pictured on art pieces were meant for adults, as well as children. By the 17th and 18th centuries, toys were available for children of the wealthy. In the early years of the 19th century, storybooks with a moral or death as a theme were produced for children. Later, dolls, doll houses and toy soldiers joined instructive toys such as jigsaw puzzles, travel games and cards. Dominoes and building blocks that could be put together and taken apart were advocated by medical advisers. By the late 19th century, middle-class children were surrounded by toys. Mass-produced toys were now affordable for middle-class parents. Dolls and toy soldiers shared space with bicycles, games, doll carriages, books and tops in the family home (Schorsch, 1979).

Children of the Poor

Although the last decades of the 19th century were prosperous for the nation as a whole, not all populations shared in the prosperity. Children of the poor and most minority children lived less comfortable and secure childhoods in the period known as the Progressive Era. While advocates for the improvement of conditions for children worked diligently to pass legislation to control child labor, regulate adoption and provide assistance for poor families, actual passage and enforcement of laws were slow and difficult.

Child Labor. By the turn of the century, laws regulating child labor had been enacted for 50 years to reduce the number of hours worked each day, increase the minimum age for full-time employment and require school attendance for all children. Until the end of the Civil War, however, enforcement of child labor laws was inconsistent. By the late 1800s, forces working against child labor were gathering strength. The labor movement, the growth of public education and social reform were strong enough to overcome manufacturers and employers who fought against losing children as resources for cheap labor (Datta, 1976).

Although these forces against the continuation of child labor were having an impact on the elimination of child labor, the battle was not easily won. Children were still employed by the hundreds of thousands in hazardous occupations. Hunter (1904), who opposed child labor, described children in the Chicago stockyards standing ankle-deep in blood and 6-year-old children carrying newly blown glass bottles from hot ovens in glass factories.

The National Child Labor committee was founded in 1904, followed by the Children's Bureau in 1912. The Bureau provided national leadership in opposing child labor. In 1916, Congress passed the Keatings-Owen Act, the first federal child labor law. Although the law was declared unconstitutional two years later, another effort in 1919 was launched when the federal government imposed a surtax on employers of child labor. This law was also declared unconstitutional in 1922.

Compulsory education laws, mandating that children would attend school, were somewhat more effective in

IMMIGRANT FAMILIES IN PENNSYLVANIA IN 1900

August's rich heat baked the First Ward relentlessly, one hot, clear-skied day after another. Kracha, sprawled on a bed that grew sticky with his sweat, gasped for air and in wakeful sleep kept confusing the buzzing of flies with sounds from the mill. Freight trains shook the house with the rhythmic double thump of their trucks over a cocked joint some thirty feet from his pillow; cinders rattled against the window, smoke and dust sifted through the curtains. Anna, suffering from prickly heat, whimpered endlessly in the kitchen.

More stupefied than rested, it was almost with a sense of relief that he heard Elena start up the stairs to call him, to tell him it was time to go to work.

The two boarders who were also working night turn that week had already left when Kracha stepped out of the house. Elena followed him, wiping her hands on her apron. She asked a child playing near by if she'd seen Alice and the child said no, she hadn't, but Mary was over by the stables. Elena lifted her head and yelled, and down by the soap factory and the stables a dark-dressed, black-stockinged figure stopped running. Her voice reached them as from a great distance. "What do you want?"

"Go to the store."
"I can't go now. Make Alice go."
"Come here!"
"I can't. I'm it."
"Stop yelling your lungs out," Kracha said. "What does the brat mean, she is it?"
"Some game they play."

Beside them the house was row of windows and doorways stretching off on either side in diminishing perspective, washtubs hanging beside every other door. From within came the common household sounds, men and women talking, babies crying. The barren, filled-in ground on which the house stood seemed lifted above the river by its sheer drop to the water's edge where the company had built up the bank by pouring molten slag. The hill on the other side of the river was a dusty green. A rowboat was crossing from the direction of Kenny's Grove. Over to the right, past the comparatively new wire works, the sun was sliding toward the hills back of Homestead. The smoke and dust there would turn it into an enormous crimson disk. – Thomas Bell. (1976). *Out of this furnace* (pp. 49-50). Pittsburgh, PA: The University of Pittsburgh Press.

removing children from employment. Mississippi, the last state to enact a compulsory education law, passed such legislation in 1918; nevertheless, child labor still continued due to inconsistent enforcement of the laws. It was not until the 1930s, when the Great Depression caused competition for employment, that strong steps were taken to end child labor. The Fair Labor Standards Act (1938) finally established national minimum standards for child labor that were accompanied by methods for enforcement. The minimum age for full employment was set at 16 years of age. Eighteen occupations were identified as too hazardous for children under the age of 16 (Datta, 1976).

In 1915, New England cotton mills still employed extended families, mostly French Canadian immigrants. The age of employed children was 16 or older; and unmarried young adults, particularly girls, continued to work in the mills and contribute to the family income. This family system of employment lasted until the 1930s (Sudia, 1976).

Foster Family Care and Adoption. The practice of placing orphans and children of destitute immigrant families in foster homes was common in the mid 1800s. This practice produced concerns; however, the New York Children's Aid Society sent children West and South to frontier areas to live with rural farm families. But when the frontier movement ended, farming became mechanized and the need for children as farm laborers was eliminated. There was also concern from the Roman Catholic Church over placing Irish children in non-Catholic homes. In addition, the New York Children's Aid Society was criticized for exercising little responsibility for selection of foster homes and their supervision following children's placement. By 1900, foster children were placed closer to home and were supervised by professional social workers.

The expansion of foster homes was affected by the closing of almshouses and other institutions for housing poor children. The 1888 National Conference of Corrections and Charities advocated the use of foster families rather than institutionalizing children. The first White House Conference on Children also supported the use of carefully selected foster homes rather than institutional placement (Datta, 1976).

Before 1851, there were no laws concerning adoption. By 1929, every state had passed some type of legislation regarding adoption. Nevertheless, there was opportunity for abuse of the system; procedures for selecting suitable adoptive homes were informal or nonexistent. In the early years of adoption practices, children were frequently sold for adoption. In other instances, individuals charged high fees for placing or locating children for placement. Although Michigan law required a judge to investigate an adoptive home before finalizing an adoption, and Minnesota passed the first law requiring detailed investigation of an adoptive home in 1917, many states had no such regulations (Datta, 1976). In fact, a court case in 1925 involved an adopted child who was sold to parents who abused her sexually (Kadushin, 1974).

Between 1890 and 1930, some positive changes were occurring for care of orphans and children with destitute parents. Foster care subsidized by the states, improvement of adoption laws and lower incidences of adult deaths reduced the numbers of true orphans. At the same time, the population of poor children with a destitute parent increased. Many of these children were served by foster family care; however, the numbers of such children continued to rise beyond the ability of foster systems to serve them.

By 1930, thousands of children lived in families who were economically unable to care for them. The Great Depression added substantially to these numbers. During that decade, federal legislation to provide assistance to destitute families signaled a shift to a concern for all children of the poor, not just orphans and children of destitute widows. The emphasis changed from enabling the poor to survive, often through the use of their own labor, to direct services such as adoption and financial support to stabilize family income in times of crisis (Datta, 1976). These public assistance services, initiated during the depression years, have continued in the final decade of the 20th century to assist increasing numbers of families in poverty.

Health Conditions

Concern about child health and the high infant death rate was not a new issue in 1890. State health departments had been established after the Civil War, and the foundation of the field of pediatrics signaled future research in child development and improved training for physicians. Although infant deaths had dropped by 1900, there were still many measures that needed to be taken to improve the survival chances for infants and children.

Between 1900 and 1910, one-third of the people who died in New York City each year were children under 5 years of age and 10 percent of those deaths were babies less than a year old (Public Health Service, 1976). Health experts were appalled with the lack of proper care and feeding of children that resulted from well-meaning but uninformed parents. A writer in the *Ladies Home Journal*, in 1904, expressed concern about mothers who would never let young children drink beer, but gave them patent medicines that might contain alcohol, opium or cocaine (Public Health Service, 1976).

The Children's Bureau was charged with investigating the causes of infant mortality, birthrates and childhood accidents and diseases. Through the efforts of the Bureau, states began to establish birth registration which facilitated the study of infant mortality and childhood deaths. These studies resulted in establishing a link between maternal health and the baby's survival chances during the first year.

Poor mothers were most likely to die as a result of childbirth; additionally, their babies were less likely to survive through the first year. Poor women delivered their own babies or depended on neighbors or untrained midwives. In 1910, untrained midwives delivered 42 percent of all the babies born in Providence, Rhode Island. A health officer in that city reported midwife practices included dressing the umbilical cord with snuff and feeding the newborn a mixture of molasses and a small child's urine (Public Health Service, 1976).

Through the efforts of Julia Lathrop, who headed the Children's Bureau, the Sheppard-Towner Act of 1921 established a federal-state program for maternal and infant health. Steps were taken to establish maternity and infant welfare centers, promote birth registration and provide educational classes for mothers and midwives. By 1927, 45 states and the Territory of Hawaii had accepted the provisions of the law. Mothers were also encouraged to become informed about the care of their infants. Through the Children's Bureau, the federal government published the first edition of *Infant Care* that offered the latest knowledge on child development and practical advice. Another booklet, *Prenatal Care*, emphasizing good nutrition and adequate medical supervision during pregnancy, had been published in 1913.

Prevention of disease in children was another concern. The source of contagious diseases in children often came from crowded living conditions in urban areas. Overcrowded city schools contributed to the spread of disease. Compulsory school attendance laws, passed in the later decades of the 19th century, added to the overcrowded conditions. To correct the problems, states began to pass school health examination laws that would exclude children with a contagious disease. Schools also had to be inspected by health inspectors to determine the condition of the school environment. Although 19 states in 1911 had passed laws or established procedures for school inspections, 29 states had made no such provisions (Public Health Service, 1976).

Throughout the period from 1890 to 1930, efforts continued to regulate milk production and sales to ensure that infants and children were supplied with milk that was safe. The beginnings of the development of antitoxins and antiseptics also contributed to the prevention of disease and illness. These practices, along with better training of physicians and nurses, benefitted children who had to be hospitalized. Previously, children contracted more serious illnesses during their hospital stay than the condition that led to their hospitalization.

Much was accomplished to improve maternal and child health within the four decades between 1890 and 1930. The efforts were impressive but did not begin to eliminate the problems contributing to childhood disease and illness. Similar efforts continue today as new sources of health problems replace those that have been controlled or eliminated.

CHILDHOOD EDUCATION: SCHOOL REFORM

Public school systems were in dire need of improvement in 1890. Cremin (1961) reported that rural schools not only were in poor condition, but instruction also had declined. They remained ungraded and children were taught by untrained teachers. Teachers continued using outdated curriculum and textbooks; moreover, recitation was the primary pedagogical method. City schools had a different set of problems. Ever growing numbers of immigrant children and migrating farm children were served in school buildings that were poorly lighted and heated and unsanitary. In some schools, class size exceeded 60 children per teacher.

The public education system faced many challenges if education was to be improved. Physical plants needed to be replaced or refurbished. The school curriculum had to be revised. Curriculum consistency between high schools and new state universities had to be determined. No longer could local school boards devise their own curriculum and hire instructors without regard for their qualifications. Teacher training needed expansion and improvement. The problem of low pay for teachers was significant. Better pay was a prerequisite to attracting better qualified teachers to the profession (Curti, 1971).

With urbanization, industrialization and universal education, the schools had a new role to play. For the first time in history, industrialization determined that children would not necessarily follow the occupations of their fathers. To qualify for new vocations in industry, students needed vocational training at the secondary level if they did not plan to continue to higher education. Schools had the additional responsibility of determining the type of secondary training that was

---

THE PLEDGE OF ALLEGIANCE

The rising tide of nationalism that swept the country in the 1890s also had an effect on the appearance of the country school and the schoolyard. In 1892 Francis Bellamy, Baptist minister and editor of the *Youth's Companion*, wrote the pledge of allegiance and set off a flurry of flag buying and flagpole raisings in thousands of little districts across the Middle Border, so that for a time the minutes of the annual meetings ran black with motions to purchase a flag and flagpole. In 1896 in the little school of District 3, Montrose Township south of Belleville in Dane County, Wisconsin, the farmers were able to restrain their enthusiasm and voted to purchase a flag no larger than three by five feet; but the year before, at the Uphoff School in the county, the farmers voted not only to buy a "six foot bunting flag staff," but to invite Cristian Uphoff to raise the flag for the first time.

In these years the flag was also being moved inside the schoolroom, which increasingly was being decorated to teach patriotism, history, and the middle-class virtues of perseverance and success. The interior of the Maple Grove School, District 8 in Berrien Township, Berrien County, Michigan, in 1887, was a typical example of how the schoolroom itself could be made to support the Midwesterners' values. On the front wall, visible to all as they entered, hung George Washington's picture, and next to it a huge "welcome" sign. On the left wall, written in large letters above the draped American flag, was the assurance that "Punctuality Brings Its Own Rewards," and prominently displayed behind the teacher's desk was the Ordinance of 1787. – Wayne E. Fuller. (1982). *The old country school* (pp. 76-77). Chicago: The University of Chicago Press.

---

appropriate for individual students.

The evolving American schools also served a social function for immigrant and transient rural children. They were expected to acculturate and assimilate students into the American culture and language. With the rapid growth of cities, the merging of many cultures and the weakening of the influence of churches and families, schools had to assume additional functions of setting standards for hygiene, correct behavior and thought in a pluralistic, democratic society (Handlin, 1976).

Whether at the elementary, secondary or university level, school became the institution for education. Whereby an educated person had been considered one who had knowledge of the classics, now an educated person was one who had been to college. Understanding of the roles and benefits of education had made a shift that affected the expectations of schools from that point forward (Graham, 1976).

Progressive Education

Progressive education was an effort to use the schools to meet the needs of an evolving urban-industrial society. It was intended to improve the lives of individuals, however diverse their background, and to replace the rigid impractical curriculum that had stagnated public education after the Civil War (Cremin, 1961). Much was expected of the public schools because, for the first time, a high level of literacy was required if graduates were to be able to make a living. As with later educational movements, the progressive education movement was unable to achieve all of its goals. The schools were expected to achieve what society could not accomplish.

Nevertheless, progressive education was a humanitarian effort to apply the promise of American life to all students. To accomplish this lofty goal, the function of the school not only had to be broadened to include concern for health, vocation and the quality of family life, but instruction had to be tailored to the varied groups of children being served. Progressives believed that culture could be democratized for all of society through compulsory school attendance.

John Dewey referred to Francis A. Parker as the father of the progressive education movement. After traveling widely in Europe after the Civil War and observing leading pedagogical innovation, Parker was committed to effecting similar changes in American education. When the school board of Quincy, Massachusetts, determined to improve the schools in that community, Parker was appointed superintendent of schools. Although not without critics, the changes in curriculum brought national attention to the Quincy schools.

Parker eventually became principal of Cook County Normal School in Chicago where he was able to implement his pedagogical techniques: child-centered and interrelated subject content to make the curriculum more meaningful for students. Art was a central component of the curriculum, while content of the subject areas was seen as a vehicle for child expression. The teacher's role was to lead children into the fields of knowledge and to extend meanings along the way (Curti, 1971).

When Dewey moved to Chicago to become a professor at the University of Chicago in 1894, his son and daughter were enrolled in the Cook County Normal School. Impressed with Parker's curriculum innovations at the school, he established the Laboratory School at the University of Chicago to test his own theories for educational change. Dewey's goal was to develop a school that could become a cooperative community while developing individual capacities at the same time. Life and its occupations should provide the basis for education, with the main test of success being the ability of individuals to meet new social situations through thoughtful action. The schoolroom should be a miniature society where the problems of a democracy are met through cooperative effort and scientific methods (Cremin, 1961; Snyder, 1972).

Dewey saw the teacher's role as guiding children toward an understanding of knowledge. The teacher should have a thorough acquaintance with organized knowledge representing the disciplines taught in the school. Theme activities integrating the content areas, rather than subject matter taught separately by discipline, were to be the basis for curriculum designed to meet the experiences and needs of students.

Dewey believed that in order to make democracy work, education had to be founded on democratic ideals and function through democratic processes. For Parker, Dewey and others, the United States had reached a point where it could move beyond European influences to develop an indigenous philosophy of education.

Reforms in Rural Education

Rural schools also felt the pressure to reform. They were expected to adopt improvements in curriculum and instruction that would replace existing practices. States passed legislation that all instruction be in English so that immigrant children would learn the new language quickly. The Palmer Method of penmanship was introduced as new emphasis was placed on handwriting skills. Country superintendents began to use standardized tests for 8th–grade graduates.

Consolidation, however, was the major reform that would ensure that rural schools would incorporate the more progressive methods. President Theodore Roosevelt formed the National Commission on Country Life that included problems in rural schools as part of its mission. It was believed that rural areas could have larger student populations with separate grades in different classrooms through consolidation efforts. Advocated by the federal government, consolidation of rural schools became a national movement.

Although rural families and communities often resisted this change because the focus of the community would be lost, pressures to conform were strong. Publications by prominent educators advocated consolidation as the answer to the needs of rural people. State legislatures provided better funding for consolidated schools, and in some states financial support was linked to compulsory school attendance laws. School administrators pushed for consolidation, recognizing that rural schools had inadequate supervision, poor financial support and below-standard curriculum. One-room schools began to close. Although it would take decades to accomplish, consolidation of rural schools was the trend that would not be reversed (Gulliford, 1984).

Reforms in Teacher Preparation

When Columbia Teachers College was chartered in 1892, it attracted Edward L. Thorndike, John Dewey, William Heard Kilpatrick and, later, Patty Smith Hill. Teachers College took a leadership role in various aspects of educational change, including the furthering of the progressive movement, the child study movement and professionalism in teacher preparation.

James Earl Russell, president of Columbia Teachers College in 1899, developed a concept of professional education that would be a guide in preparing teachers. Russell's interest in training teachers extended beyond public schooling to private schools, reform schools, hospitals, settlements and other philanthropic institutions. He made firsthand tours of southern schools during the reconstruction period following the Civil War and helped select young men and women to be trained at Teachers College (Cremin, 1961).

The work of Teachers College in training teachers, as well as that of other universities, colleges and normal schools, was desperately needed; educators began to devise means to standardize requirements for securing a teacher certificate. Despite these efforts, states had a long way to go before they demanded a college education for teachers.

Before the Civil War, women entered the teaching profession in large numbers. By 1862, the number of women teachers exceeded the number of men teachers in New Jersey. After the Civil War, other states reported similar numbers. A 1911 study reported that the typical teacher was 24 years old, female and had four years of education beyond the elementary school (Bonn, 1976).

Attempts to improve teacher preparation standards were interrupted, however, by World War I. In 1918, the National Education Association reported that half of the 600,000 teachers lacked special training; furthermore, about 20 percent were without a 10th–grade education. As late as 1926, 15 states had not set scholarship requirements for a teaching certificate. States bound teachers to petty restrictions that seemed more important than teacher training in some states.

Employment of teachers in their home towns was prohibited in Alabama, and a North Carolina county outlawed "quarreling among teachers." Between 1920 and 1930, school authorities in several communities refused to appoint teachers who bobbed their hair, painted their lips, or rouged their cheeks. Such restrictions often were embodied in state codes or written into contracts. A Virginia county school system rule still on the books in 1935 read, "Any conduct such as staying out late at night, etc., which may cause criticism of the teacher will not be tolerated by the school board." (Bonn, 1976, p. 168)

The Child Study Movement

The progressive education movement was but one source of change that would affect the course of education in the 20th century. The child study movement was to bring a totally new perspective on how children, particularly young children, should be educated. G. Stanley Hall's *The Content of Children's Minds* (1883) and Edward L. Thorndike's *Animal Intelligence* (1911), along with John Dewey's *School and Society* (1900), formed a nucleus of new ideas in science, psychology, philosophy and education that would transform educational practice. The ideas emanating from Charles Darwin's *The Origin of Species* (1859) put into place the concept of change, adaptation, development and survival, rather than the belief of fixed species. Now, society had to reconsider the religious and moral principles of the 17th and 18th centuries and its faith in a fixed and knowable truth (Weber, 1984). Darwin's theory of the evolutionary effect on growth and development, combined with new perspectives on scientific study of the nature and scope of development, resulted in a clearer understanding of the relationship between development and learning.

Edward Thorndike, influenced by the work of Binet and Simon on the measurement of intelligence, conducted observational experiments on learning at Teachers College, leading to his explanation of behavior as a matter of stimulus and response. He defined three basic laws of learning–readiness, exercise and effect–through stimulus and response connections. Thorndike's *Educational Psychology* (1910) explained his theory and its relationship to learning.

Stanley Hall, president of Clark University, established a center for child study that was followed by similar centers at other colleges and universities. Using questionnaires as a technique for gathering data, more than 100 studies related to child development were produced under his leadership (Weber, 1984). Hall's basic

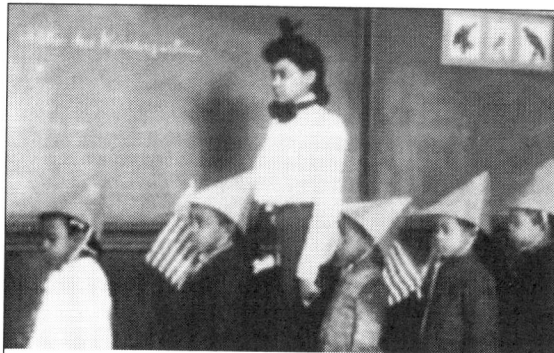

REFORMS IN BLACK EDUCATION
In the summer of 1886, at age eighteen, W. E. B. DuBois taught school in the hills of Tennessee. He was a Fisk University student then, and it was common for "Fisk men" to venture into rural Tennessee during summer vacations to gain practical experience in teaching. In a rural black community that seemed least removed from slavery DuBois found a school. He was informed that but once since the Civil War had a teacher been there. . .

Yet, undaunted by their poverty and sustained by a distinctive orientation toward learning, the parents saw to it when school opened in late July that their children attended. In the early morning, DuBois heard "the patter of little feet down the dusty road," and soon he faced a "room of dark solemn faces and bright eager eyes." "There they sat," DuBois recalled, "nearly thirty of them, on the rough benches, their faces shading from a pale cream to a deep brown, the little feet bare and swinging, the eyes full of mischief, and the hands grasping Webster's blue-back spelling book. – James D. Anderson. (1988). *The education of Blacks in the South, 1860-1935* (pp. 282-283). Chapel Hill: The University of North Carolina Press.

thesis, based on Darwinism, was that individual growth and development passed through stages similar to the stages man passed through from presavagery to civilization. From findings in his studies, Hall proposed a child-centered school curriculum based on the nature, growth and development of children (Cremin, 1961).

Arnold Gesell, one of Hall's most influential students, made his own contribution to child study through the Yale Clinic of Child Development established in 1911. His observational research focused on the maturation of the child, based on the concept of inherent or genetic predetermination. Gesell established norms of growth and development and the principle of developmental readiness for learning that was most influential in schooling after 1930.

The new scientific approach to learning had implications for schooling and became the basis for major reform in education. Other changes and development were also evolving that would affect schooling. A growing sensitivity to the needs of disabled children was resulting in better programs for this population of students. Efforts were also being made to improve education for Blacks, particularly through the work of Booker T. Washington and J. L. M. Curry. It would be after the end of WW II before major improvements would be made on behalf of these two populations of students.

Reforms in Black Education

The meager resources invested in the education of Blacks after the years of reconstruction in the South reflected the southern White attitude that Blacks should work with their hands rather than prepare for professional careers. Eight occupations accounted for 74 percent of the employed Black citizens in both the North and the South: waiter, servant, cook, barber, laborer, porter, laundress and seamstress (Gross & Gross, 1976). Although land grant colleges had been established for Black students, only those students whose parents had economic means to send them attended.

The question of what kind of education was most appropriate for Blacks in the post–Civil War economy focused on occupations that were possible. In the South, Black skilled tradesmen were thriving and forming a middle-class population. In the North, particularly in Boston, urban Blacks were joined by southern Black immigrants seeking better opportunities. Unfortunately, low occupational status, high mobility and high death rates due to poor living conditions meant that opportunities were also limited in the North.

Efforts to advance Blacks through education were funded through philanthropy. Some Black leaders advocated industrial education as a route toward progress without threatening the power structure and avoiding conflict during the post-reconstruction era (Gross & Gross, 1976). Booker T. Washington was one leader who sought to educate his people through accommodation to and compromise with the power structure. He sought dignity and respect by preparing Black people to be artisans and competent workers. Tuskegee Institute, founded by Washington in 1881, established a practical education for Blacks and successfully overcame prejudice against the education of Blacks.

J. L. M. Curry, the best known and influential figure in southern education during the period, also was a force in this movement. A traditional, White southern gentleman, devoted to the work of the Baptist Church, Curry believed industrial education would benefit Blacks. Although he had to battle more conservative southern Whites, he successfully secured funds for educating Blacks and motivated others to do the same (Curti, 1971).

While Washington believed that equality for Black people could only be achieved in the distant future, W. E. DuBois held the position that there was an equally important need for Blacks to have more immediate access to higher education. DuBois, who had earned his doctorate from Harvard, believed that Blacks who received a liberal education could help the progress of the whole Black population. He initiated the Niagara movement in 1905, to organize through protest the cause for voting rights and equality. The Niagara movement failed; but, in 1909, DuBois and other liberal Black leaders established the National Association for the Advancement of Colored People (NAACP), with a mission to pursue educational equality.

Separate but equal facilities were legally established in the railroad case of Plessy vs. Ferguson. A 1908 Kentucky statute that required separate instruction for Blacks and Whites was upheld in court. School segregation was made legal, and the NAACP's efforts to assure that separate facilities were equal in quality of education usually failed. When cases of inequality were tried, the courts usually ruled that inequality had not been properly demonstrated (Gross & Gross, 1976). The battle for educational equality was not to be achieved until much later.

Education of Disabled Children

Alexander Graham Bell proposed to the 1898 convention of the National Education Association that programs for the disabled be established in the public schools. In addition to being an inventor, Dr. Bell was also a speech therapist.

He was not the first to advocate education for disabled children. Thomas Hopkins Gallaudet, a teacher, visited a school for the deaf in Paris. Using the information he learned in France, he established the American Asylum for the Deaf in West Hartford, Connecticut, in 1817. In 1826, Dr. John D. Fisher persuaded the Massachusetts State Legislature to vote funds to establish the New England Asylum for the Blind in Boston, which became the Perkins School for the Blind. Anne Sullivan, Helen Keller's teacher, was a graduate of Perkins Institute,

as was Laura Bridgman who was both blind and deaf. In 1871, a day school for severely hearing–impaired students was also established in Boston, followed by a class for mentally retarded children in Providence in 1896 and a school for physically disabled children in Chicago four years later.

Elizabeth Farrell, a public school teacher in New York City, demonstrated how disabled children should be taught as individuals and according to their disabilities in public schools. She organized an ungraded class for children who were considered to be "misfits." Later, she organized classes for younger children who were mentally retarded and trade classes for older retarded children. In 1922, she organized the Council for Exceptional Children and served as its first president. The Council was concerned with exceptionally gifted children, as well as the physically, mentally and emotionally disabled (Gross & Gross, 1976).

EARLY CHILDHOOD EDUCATION: EXPANSION AND CHANGE

The last decades of the 19th century were years of great growth for kindergarten education. Associations were organizing to extend these efforts. Public school kindergartens were growing in number, although the settlement kindergartens continued to be established to serve destitute children and their mothers. The humanitarian interest in providing programs for poor children had led to a view that Froebel's Gifts and Occupations were an appropriate curriculum for the new emphasis on industrial education these children would need when they were older (Weber, 1969). Teachers in settlement kindergartens, however, found the Froebelian Program difficult to maintain in light of the problems with which children lived and the lack of appropriate classroom settings for classes at urban settlement locations.

Influence of Scientific Thinking

While teachers of philanthropic kindergarten programs found it necessary to change the curriculum to fit their children's needs, the kindergarten movement as a whole was engaged in a controversy over the direction it should take because of the new scientific emphases currently affecting reform in the public schools. Progressive kindergartens were strongly affected by Hall, Dewey and Thorndike and the implications of their research for how kindergarten teachers should plan and implement instruction.

As a result of his work on early development, Hall proposed that more attention be given to children's health problems, as well as recommending that the curriculum be child centered and based on the stages of development. Dewey believed that activities for children must promote psychological continuity of growth. Work for the young child should be constructive, with young children learning to think by managing their own experiences and solving problems related to new situations. Dewey was critical of Froebelian methods whereby children imitated teacher directions. Constructive work, including field trips, music, nature study and gardening, should use activities related to the child's out-of-school life. Social interaction was important, as was the perception of the class as a miniature community (Cremin, 1969). Thorndike related his psychological laws of stimulus-response learning to kindergarten, where children should form acceptable habits through use of concrete objects, in imaginative play and following appropriate social forms (Weber, 1969).

Although Dewey and Thorndike are both associated with progressive education, their philosophy about the purposes of education and instructional methods differed. Thorndike focused on educational research and practice based on measurement of learning. Dewey, on the other hand, was concerned with the interests and talents possessed by children and how school could foster a cooperative community in which children could develop their individual potential. These two approaches to progressivism resulted in a struggle between child-centered education and a more scientific basis for education supported by educational testing. These two positions on the best approach for educating young children persist to the present day.

Progressive Kindergarten Programs

Kindergartens were already breaking with traditional Froebelian methods. Anna Bryan viewed the kindergarten as a laboratory for vitalizing teaching practices. Eudora Hailmann divorced herself from rigid Froebelian practices by introducing a sand table, doll house and enlarged forms of building gifts into her classroom. Alice Putnam, influenced by Colonel Francis Parker and Jane Addams, used science and art with young children (Snyder, 1972; Weber, 1969).

As new sources of philosophical and psychological thought and work became understood, kindergarten educators entered a period of confusion and controversy about curriculum practices. The progressives embraced the newer influences, while the conservatives held on to Froebelian methods. Some progressives made minor modifications in the Froebelian curriculum, while others abandoned it altogether.

Many programs incorporated Hall's recommendation for freedom of movement and scheduled periods of free play with seesaws, swings, dolls, toy dishes,

---

FREEDOM FOR PUPILS; RELAXATION FOR TEACHERS
By Mr. Kerr, Superintendent, Kirkwood, Mo.

In our schools we have emphasized activity. Every boy and girl in the grades is given 30 minutes to play in the morning and 30 minutes play in the afternoon during school hours, under intelligent direction. There is freedom in the school both for the children and for the teachers. The boys and girls can go about the building with exactly the same freedom you teachers have in this hotel. It is no sin if boys and girls talk to each other. If you make a rigid system where the boy and the girl are under a police system, there is not relaxation.

Every grade teacher has two periods of relaxation during the day. In the upper grades the teachers get three 30-minute periods for that purpose. As a result, we have better teachers. We are not doing that for the teachers only; we are doing it for the boys and girls, for by this plan we have a set of teachers who are at their best all the time. – National Council of Primary Education. Report of the Second Annual Meeting at Kansas City, Mo., February 27, 1917 and the Third Annual Meeting at Atlantic City, N.J., February 26, 1918. Department of the Interior, Bureau of Education. Bulletin 1918, No. 26.

DISCUSSION OF DELEGATES
Miss Faddis of St. Paul

It behooves us all to see what we can do to make a freer atmosphere. I went into a room a few years ago where the children were sitting in straight rows. I was examining the lower grades in phonics, and was giving exercises to test the children, or asking the teachers to do so. In this case the teacher thought the exercise would be more orthodox if she gave it, so she called the children up to the board, and when they were there in a straight row she told them to do just what they were told to do. Then she began using the phonic "im" and they said "grim," prim," etc., and then took their seats; I could not bear to leave the room without finding out whether these children could be anything but grim and prim, so I began to talk to them about the sounds I heard on my way to school that morning, and about the chickens. I did not have a sound of response when I asked them if they had any chickens at home, and finally I said, "You know what chickens say, don't you?" There was no response, and the teacher said, "They do not; they have not been informed." – National Council of Primary Education. Third Annual Meeting at Atlantic City, NJ, February 26, 1918. Department of the Interior, Bureau of Education. Bulletin 1918, No. 26.

---

beanbags, sand piles and garden tools. Directed work was changed to free choice, while traditional games were replaced by dramatic play. Social development following John Dewey's ideas was stressed in other kindergartens. In Dewey's own sub-primary program, constructive work with blocks and raw materials was used to engage in realistic activities of the home and community. Still another kindergarten curriculum model, called an industrial program, emphasized neighborhood occupations using Froebelian materials.

Influence of the Child Study Movement

The findings from Hall's child studies had a direct impact on the move away from the Froebelian curriculum. It was learned, for example, that large muscle development preceded small muscle development; therefore, Froebelian materials requiring fine motor skills were inappropriate. Larger building blocks, dolls, a playhouse with kitchen utensils and toy animals were recommended by Alice Temple. Drawing, painting, and clay modeling became the child's expression instead of teacher-directed Froebelian occupations stressing preciseness of the production (Weber, 1969).

These are a few examples of innovations implemented by teachers recognizing the need to match curriculum practices with the child's development. As the new scientific approach to curriculum gained wider acceptance and more research was conducted, the process of curriculum reform in the kindergarten continued.

Kindergarten-Primary Conflict

Kindergarten increasingly became part of public school systems between 1900 and 1925. At that time, primary grades had not yet incorporated curriculum modifications resulting from the new ideas in educational philosophy and psychology. This resulted in debate between kindergarten programs based on new studies in child development and progressive education and primary education with a predetermined curriculum implemented through recitation and drill. The hope of those supporting progressive kindergartens was to effect changes in primary curriculum to make it more like kindergarten curriculum.

Primary teachers held a different view. From their perspective, the role of the

Boston Herald April 24, 1902

kindergarten program was to prepare children for 1st grade. A need for continuity was agreed upon, but the nature of the continuity was the source of disagreement between the two groups. Addressing delegates to the 9th annual meeting of the International Kindergarten Union in Boston, Superintendent Edwin Seaver of the Boston Public Schools summarized the problem:

> Ever since the kindergarten became an important factor in public education we have heard and read much about the need of closer relations between the kindergarten and primary schools. Sometimes we hear the primary school criticized because it, or the lower part of it does not become itself a kindergarten. On the other hand, we hear the kindergarten criticized because it does not take on more the traditional character of a primary school. (Boston Herald, April, 24, 1902)

The conflict between these two views was eased as public schools modified their curriculum as a result of school reform. Improvements in teacher training for both kindergarten and elementary school teachers provided preparation for teaching that was more similar. Professionalization of education and movement toward certification for teachers resulted in growth of training programs in colleges and normal schools, with a corresponding decline in independent kindergarten programs. By 1930, at least 80 percent of teacher training institutions combined the preparation of kindergarten and primary teachers. Prominent kindergarten proponents led university efforts to improve kindergarten-primary education and training. Patty Smith Hill, who had studied under Anna Bryan, became a member of the faculty at Columbia Teachers College, while Alice Temple led the kindergarten-primary unit at the University of Chicago.

RUTH BURRITT

Ruth Burritt was another person who played an important part in arousing public interest in kindergartens. Miss Burritt, elementary school teacher, had first become interested in Froebel's teachings from observing a kindergarten in Wisconsin. Realizing her need for training if she was to pursue the new work, she went East for study and later took a position as a kindergartener in Boston. When it was decided to have a demonstration kindergarten at the Philadelphia Centennial Exposition, Miss Burritt was appointed as teacher upon the recommendation of the Froebel Society of Boston. Under her direction the kindergarten soon became one of the most popular features of the fair. The tiny pupils, who were orphans from the Northern Home for Friendless Children, were brought to the exhibition grounds three days a week for demonstration sessions. The rest of the time Miss Burritt lived at the orphanage with them and succeeded in causing several reforms to be carried out at the institution. During the demonstration sessions the children went through a typical kindergarten routine, with songs, marching, games, and periods devoted to handicrafts. Thousands of visitors thronged past to watch them and to listen to Miss Burritt's explanations of the Froebelian system. As the result of the interest aroused by the demonstrations, kindergartens were started for the first time in many communities throughout the United States. – E. L. Thornborough. (1956). Eliza A. Baker, Her life and work. Indianapolis: The Eliza A. Baker Club, Inc. and the Indiana Historical Society.

Nursery School Movement and Other Early Childhood Programs

While the kindergarten movement was serving increasing numbers of 5-year-old children, the nursery school movement was established to serve children under the age of 5. The nursery school concept originated in England under the leadership of Rachel and Margaret McMillan, who desired to provide physical care under healthful conditions for poor children. English nursery schools soon incorporated the psychoanalytic thinking of Freud and Jung.

In the United States, nursery schools began because of research in child development. The Ruggles Street Nursery School in Boston, established in 1920, was funded as a philanthropic effort. The new child development research centers at colleges and universities also established nursery classrooms in laboratory school settings. By 1926, such nursery schools were operating at Columbia Teachers College, Johns Hopkins, Yale, Iowa University, Merrill-Palmer School for Homemaking and University of Minnesota. Over the years, the movement spread as universities across the United States established nursery schools and child development centers for research, teacher training and curriculum development (Weber, 1969).

Simultaneously, other early childhood educators were conducting experimental programs according to their own vision of desirable innovations in preschool education. Two such schools were established by Caroline Pratt and Margaret Naumberg.

Caroline Pratt's play schools in several New York City locations became known as the City and Country School. Originating from a desire to do something for the poor, the school eventually enrolled children from 3 to 13 and included a summer camping program. The program was based on firsthand experiences and individual expression on the part of students. Academic subjects were postponed until students were 7 years old. These subjects were learned through play and child-initiated investigations.

The Walden School, established by Margaret Naumberg in 1915, applied Freud's theory of analytic psychology. Naumberg's intention was to create an environment that would facilitate the release of children's unconscious emotional life into personal expression. She rejected behaviorism and Dewey's social cooperativeness in favor of individual personality (Weber, 1969).

Such individual efforts to develop early childhood programs were joined by many other approaches, including short-lived Montessori programs and schools with behaviorist curricula. As the field of psychology and child development produced additional research knowledge, the field of early childhood education continued to respond and incorporate new information into various program models.

INTERNATIONAL KINDERGARTEN UNION: BEGINNINGS OF ASSOCIATION FOR CHILDHOOD EDUCATION INTERNATIONAL

"I think that one of the most distinct remembrances is that one of the ladies who sat on the platform, sat with her knees crossed and swinging one foot. I was horrified because I had been taught that ladies kept their feet on the floor. I rather think that in spite of the years that have passed, I still hold somewhat to the same idea." – From a letter from Fannie Smith, charter member of the International Kindergarten Union, to Mary Leeper, Executive Secretary, October 10, 1941, describing the first IKU meeting.

When the 30 charter members of the International Kindergarten Union met in 1892 at the Baptist Church in Saratoga Springs, New York, the kindergarten movement already had a successful history in the United States. Philanthropic, parochial and public school kindergartens had been established in all sections of the country. Training schools had been organized to train kindergarten teachers. As the numbers of kindergartens expanded, educators began to form associations for mutual support and advancement of their cause. Between 1880 and 1890, kindergarten departments were added at normal schools. Ruth Burritt conducted a demonstration kindergarten at the 1876 Centennial Exposition in Philadelphia. As a result of the interest aroused by the Exposition, kindergartens and kindergarten associations increased even more. During this same period, kindergartens made rapid progress in their acceptance in public school systems (Association for Childhood Education, 1937).

Recognition of the relevance of kindergartens as part of public school systems was validated in 1884 when a

ONE OF THE FIRST QUESTIONNAIRES SENT TO IKU BRANCHES ST. LOUIS CONFERENCE, 1897

To Branches and Members of IKU:

There has been so much discussion in reference to the right *size* and *use* of Kindergarten materials that it seems desirable to get a consensus of opinions from within our own ranks.

Will you therefore kindly help us to an intelligent discussion of the matter by answering *very soon* the following questions, giving to many the results of your own observations and experience? A report based on these returns will be made at the St. Louis meeting April 19th, 20th, 21st. Presidents and officers of Branches are requested to circulate these papers among individual members, or to make the questions topics at regular meetings.

1. Do you think it desirable to enlarge the 1*st*, 2*nd*, 3*rd*, 4*th* and 5*th* gifts? Reasons.
2. Do you use stick-laying? How? Objections, if any.
3. Do you follow a sequence of games? Illustrate your method.
4. What games do you find most valuable? Where do you find them?
5. Do you use the Froebel drawing? Reasons *pro* and *con*.
6. What do you sew? Materials used.
7. Do you use perforating? Reasons *pro* and *con*.
8. Do you use the Mother Play in your kindergarten?
9. Do you use a programme? How do you make it?
10. Have you found any help from Child-Study literature and discussions? What have you done in this direction?

Please send your answers to any or all of these questions to Lucy Wheelock, 284 Dartmouth St., Boston, or to Corresponding Secretary—Sara E. Wiltse, W. Roxbury, Mass.

THE KINDERGARTEN AS A PREPARATION FOR THE HIGHEST CIVILIZATION

The child from four to six years of age, the proper age for the kindergarten, has not yet hardened himself through the influence of the slum or through the influence of a too indulgent education in the nursery of the rich family, so as to be beyond the hope of cure through the school. The kindergarten is for this reason the most potent of all the instrumentalities used to overcome the influence of the slums which exist in our cities. Urban life is increasing all over the land and it is the natural effect of urban life to concentrate in certain quarters of the city the weaklings of society. The slum has been called the menace to civilization. It is certainly the menace to local self-government and political freedom.

As a matter of self-preservation each city should organize a strong force of kindergartens throughout all precincts where the weaklings of society come together.

Viewed in this special function of usefulness, Froebel's kindergarten is a great blessing to civilization, and for this and much else Froebel's name is to be celebrated as one of the great apostles of humanity. – W. T. Harris. From a paper read at the annual meeting of the International Kindergarten Union, Pittsburgh, PA, April 16, 1903.

kindergarten unit was added to the National Education Association. It was at an earlier meeting of NEA that the kindergarten educators decided to form their own organization and extend their work more effectively. The aims of the new organization were:

- To gather and disseminate knowledge of the kindergarten movement throughout the world.
- To bring into active cooperation all kindergarten interests.
- To promote the establishment of kindergartens.
- To elevate the standard of professional training of kindergarteners. (Smith, 1942, p. 84)

One of the first projects of this NEA unit was to make plans for presenting a model kindergarten at the Columbian Exposition in Chicago, in 1893. The International Kindergarten Union held a meeting at the Exposition, followed by a meeting of the International Congress of Education under NEA auspices. At these meetings, papers were read and addresses given concerning the progress of the kindergarten movement as well as problems associated with the establishment of kindergartens.

At the dinner meeting of NEA, IKU decided to hold meetings apart from NEA and the National Council of Women with which it was also affiliated. Subsequently, IKU met as a separate organization for the first time at Teachers College, New York City, in February 1896. In the years to follow, the organization continued to develop and grow and quickly became involved in issues surrounding the school reform movement (Smith, 1942).

IKU: An International Organization

From its inception, the new kindergarten association was intended to be an international organization with the primary objective of gathering and disseminating information about the kindergarten movement. One of the original charter members, Ada Marean Hughes, was a pioneer in the establishment of kindergartens in Canada. She and her husband, James L. Hughes, a Toronto educator, were frequent speakers at IKU meetings. In 1905, IKU held its annual meeting in Toronto. The following year, Ada Hughes, a conservative Froebelian, was elected president of the organization. She maintained a leadership position in IKU until her death in 1929 (Dixon, 1991).

By 1924, IKU had branches in Canada, England, China and Japan. There were 15 state branches in the United States, 1 territorial branch in Hawaii and 132 local branches in 30 states with over 25,000 members. Members of foreign branches attended the annual conferences as delegates (International Kindergarten Union, 1924). A photograph from the 1926 conference included delegates from Mexico.

Controversy Between Froebelian and Progressive Kindergarteners

By the time IKU was organized, school reform had already begun. The new school of scientific pedagogy was making an impact on public schools and it was inevitable that kindergarten educators would become involved.

The controversy between those who adhered to Froebelian principles and those who were more progressive was initiated at the annual IKU conference in Chicago in 1895. G. Stanley Hall addressed the "new psychology" in the opening address. Thirty-three of the 35 leading kindergarteners in attendance were offended by Hall's comments on the unsoundness of Froebel's methodology and left the meeting. The two who remained, Anna E. Bryan and Patty Smith Hill, became leaders in the progressive kindergarten movement (Snyder, 1972). For the remainder of the 1890s and into the first decades of the 1900s, the membership of the IKU struggled through their own resolution of the reconstruction of the kindergarten program.

Concerns about the kindergarten curriculum became the core of conference meetings. Interest in the meetings brought new membership and active participation at the conferences. Heated debates were held at the annual meetings about the use of symbolism, free play, the appropriate amount of teacher direction and the role of creative activity. With each succeeding year, the differences between liberals and conservatives escalated (Weber, 1964).

In 1895, a Child Study Committee was organized by IKU. Within committee reports and discussions at IKU meetings, liberals and conservatives debated their views (Smith, 1942). In 1903, a Committee of Fifteen was established to formulate a statement about contemporary thought. Expanded to the Committee of Nineteen, the committee members found it necessary to issue three reports in 1909: a liberal report, a conservative report and a report representing a moderate view. The three rewritten reports were published in book form (Committee of Nineteen, 1913).

Regardless of original positions, members of IKU were embracing the results of scientific research. Through continued reports, discussions, debates and exchanges of ideas, IKU played a leadership role in the continuous evolution of kindergarten programs.

Expansion of International Kindergarten Union

Songs for Delegates Day
(To the Tune of 'Over There')

Baltimore! Baltimore!
Here we are, here we are Baltimore!
East and West are humming,
North and South are coming,
The Kindergartners come from everywhere–
Baltimore! Baltimore!
We will share in your schools if we may,
We will work with you and play with you,
And we won't go back 'till you tell us we may stay.

World War I changed the focus of IKU. In 1918, the impact of a world war was addressed. A Committee of Nineteen was organized in connection with children in the war zones, with a subcommittee undertaking the task of protecting and serving America's children as well.

A kindergarten unit in France was established to serve refugee children in war zones and other areas affected by the war. The organization helped raise the funds needed to send Fanniebell Curtis, Kindergarten Director in New York City, to organize these kindergartens and a training school for teachers in France (International Kindergarten Union, 1924; Smith, 1942).

The Board met in Washington, D. C. for its Christmas session (1924). The usual business was completed on the last day of the year when the members returned to their homes with the exception of Miss Boyce and Miss Greenwood (Ella Ruth Boyce was President, 1924-25). They remained to make further investigations about selecting Headquarters for the organization and to attend the President's New Year's Reception.

A heavy snowstorm New Year's Eve caused difficulties in getting about on New Year's morning. After going from place to place investigating "Headquarters" we suddenly realized time had slipped by and the closing hour for the White House reception was about to end. As there was no time to return to the hotel to get properly attired, to get a taxi, etc., we went as we were—galoshes and all—saying no one would notice us in the crowd; we walked bravely in to the strains of the Marine Band and found a single couple awaiting us; we thought this the advanced guard to take us to the President and Mrs. Coolidge. As we drew nearer, however, we realized we were having (to our amazement) a private reception with the President and his wife—the crowd had gone before—we were the last. But how gracious they were stepping out and remarking "How glad we are to see you—" "How good of you to come," etc. We were then ushered into the Blue Room where we found the crowd assembled. It was really quite a delightful experience; we were not made to feel humiliated in the least by being the last. We then went to our hotel, had luncheon, dressed, took a taxi and attended the reception in proper style given by Mr. and Mrs. Herbert Hoover. Here all the flowers, fruits, and the tempting viands on the tea table were from California so I, in particular, felt at home. – From a letter from Barbara Greenwood to Mary Leeper, Executive Secretary, May 19, 1941.

IKU continued to expand, taking an active interest in the issues of the day. The Committee on Child Study reviewed research about child growth and development and organized information about the use of tests with kindergarten children. A Literature Committee was appointed to compile a list of stories and poetry suitable for kindergarten and primary children. The first issue of the *Journal of Childhood Education* was published in 1924 "so as to give greater assistance to teachers of young children" (International Kindergarten Union, 1924, p. 2). This and subsequent publications were to increase the significant impact of the organization in the field of early childhood education.

At this convention (Minneapolis, 1924) I was elected President, and inherited a plan, endorsed by the delegate body, to develop an official journal. This was the outstanding achievement of my administration. I felt at the time that it was perhaps a case of rushing in where wiser folks might hesitate, but I still believe firmly that without such unconsidered rashness, little progress is made. We were fortunate in securing the cooperation of the publishing firm of Williams and Wilkins, who were really very generous in many respects. At least we must remember them gratefully in that they made the start possible.

We were unfortunate in securing the ill-will and rather amused contempt of the man in authority at Milton Bradley's. I made a personal trip to Springfield, Massachusetts, to confer with him, and hoped to get some cooperation. Perhaps the fact that I had a very black eye, caused by an automobile wreck, influenced him against what we were trying to do. At any rate, he thought we were a bunch of women with little knowledge of the publishing business, as no doubt we were, but he overlooked our vision. He promised to present our request for some cooperative action to the Board of his company, but I have never felt that it was adequately done. – From a letter from Ella Ruth Boyce to Mary Leeper, Executive Secretary (no date).

CHAPTER 3
A WORLD IN DEPRESSION AND WAR: 1930-1950

After the end of World War I, the United States had a decade of expansion and prosperity. Business prospered as new management and production techniques resulted in a rise in mass–produced consumer goods. The introduction of electricity into factories and rural areas brought progress that affected all categories of the economy. Corporation mergers resulted in even larger industries such as DuPont, General Electric and General Motors. The invention of the automobile revolutionized transportation, while radios and movies provided American people with common experiences and a shared culture. Shorter working hours increased the time available for leisure activities and the automobile made possible family excursions.

National advertising on the radio and in popular magazines, combined with installment plans for consumer credit, brought acquisition of new consumer products within the reach of the middle– and working–class populations. A new concept, shopping centers, offered a different type of shopping experience in suburban areas. Highway construction and gasoline production encouraged this as well as vacation trips.

Americans were not willing to share prosperity with all populations, however. Quotas were established to restrict immigration of undesirable people. Prejudice against Jewish groups spread through anti-Semitic efforts. The Klu Klux Klan harassed Blacks and immigrants who were Catholic or Jewish. Klan activities included nightriding, arson and other forms of intimidation.

Prohibition was legislated to control the use of alcohol, but any reduction was temporary. Liquor was smuggled successfully, allowing speakeasies and illegal saloons to flourish. New York City had an estimated 30,000 speakeasies during prohibition (Henretta et al., 1987).

When the stock market crashed in 1929, it touched off the Great Depression that would not end until the country was mobilized for the effort to win World War II. By 1932, more than 25 percent of the nation's workers were unemployed. Government initiatives under

---

FRANKLIN DELANO ROOSEVELT'S THOUGHTS
ON THE GREAT DEPRESSION

This is pre-eminently the time to speak the truth, the whole truth, frankly and boldly. Nor need we shrink from honestly facing conditions in our country today. The great nation will endure as it has endured, will revive and will prosper.

So first of all let me assert my firm belief that the only thing we have to fear is fear itself–nameless, unreasoning, unjustified terror which paralyzes needed efforts to convert retreat into advance. . .

In such a spirit on my part and on yours we face our common difficulties. They concern, thank God, only material things. Values have shrunken to fantastic levels, taxes have risen; our ability to pay has fallen; government of all kinds is faced by serious curtailment of income, the means of exchange are frozen in the currents of trade, the withered leaves of industrial enterprise lie on every side; farmers find no market for their produce; the savings of many years in thousands of families are gone. – From Franklin Delano Roosevelt's First Inaugural Address, March 4, 1933. In Richard Hofstadler & Beatrice K. Hofstadler (Eds.), (1969). *Great issues in American history, Volume III* (p.344). New York: Vintage Books.

DEPRESSION IN THE SOUTH

As the depression continued, waves of people roamed the country in search of work. Men left home, hoping to land jobs and then send for their wives and children. In other cases entire families packed up their automobiles and head west or north. Large tracts of land fell under the hammer of foreclosure, and banks, mortgage companies, life insurance companies, and other lenders took over the land. Hoover carts, made from automobile axles and tires and pulled by horses or mules, carried people about, for they were too poor to buy gasoline or license tags. Herbert Hoover, who had first earned international attention for organizing relief abroad and then ran the relief effort during the 1927 Mississippi River flood, watched helplessly as the economy unwound. Ultimately, the Reconstruction Finance Corporation loaned funds to corporations, but for the poor, Hoover had no imaginative program, no lifeline. Dispossessed, broken-spirited, and searching for jobs, many people hoped for economic recovery or for a leader who could offer a bold program. Until this time, in the minds of most people, government aid seemed alien, even socialistic, but as hard times continued, there was no other hope. Federal intrusion, so long feared, offered their only salvation. – Pete Daniel. (1986). *Standing at the crossroads* (pp. 111-112). New York: Hill & Wang.

President Franklin Delano Roosevelt to provide relief for the unemployed restored the nation's confidence. At the same time, the New Deal resulted in an enlarged, bureaucratic government that set a precedent for the expectation of social and economic benefits through federal resources. During the 1930s, more than a third of the population received some type of government assistance, including farm loans, Social Security or government funded work programs. In spite of these government efforts, hardships of the Great Depression continued for more than a decade.

Depression meant hard times during mass unemployment. People who had been poor during the 1920s were joined by working-class and middle-class people who were out of work or worked at lower paying jobs that allowed them to subsist. Old people who lost their life savings when the banks failed shared hardship with the wealthy who lost all of their invested wealth in the stock market crash.

Farmers in the Great Plains suffered the effects of a severe drought during the same decade. The plains states were known as the Dust Bowl because of the extensive dust storms that decimated farms over a wide area. Farm families who lost their land migrated West where workers were still used in the fields. They found more migrant workers in California, however, than opportunities for employment. Wages were very low and, at best, only occasional employment became available. Discouraged by the lack of employment and the severe drought in the Midwest, many young people left their families and became boy and girl hoboes (Henretta et al., 1987; Reynolds, 1976).

The Japanese bombing of Pearl Harbor on December 7, 1941 had the same magnitude of effect on the United States as the crash of the stock market in 1929. The country entered a global war that ended the Great Depression and returned the nation to prosperity. The federal government expanded in size and influence as industrial resources were mobilized to produce goods, food and equipment for the war. Social changes occurred as women took jobs in defense industries or took their families and followed their husbands to their assignment in the military forces. The labor movement strengthened its position because scarcity of workers and the growing demand for laborers allowed unions to negotiate for better pay and working conditions.

The United States also took a leadership role in international affairs. President Roosevelt worked with heads of state and other government leaders in planning wartime strategies. With final Allied victory in 1945, President Truman and the presidents who followed maintained a worldwide leadership position in the postwar reconstruction of Europe and Japan.

CHILDHOOD IN THE UNITED STATES: 1930-1950

Family Life and the American Culture During Depression and War

The decades of the 1930s and 1940s were years of coping, first with economic problems and then with the hardships of a nation at war. Both periods forced people to be resourceful and to modify their style of living. During the depression years, families tried to maintain their self-respect and keep their lives as normal as possible. The knowledge that the whole country was struggling with the economic downturn made it easier for families to retain their dignity and maintain hope for a better future.

Children often reacted less negatively than their parents to the downward mobility their family experienced. Although variation in their diet might have been more restricted, most children did not suffer severe food deprivation. Their parents may have worried or felt bitter about their economic situation, but children would remember those years as a happy time within the family unit.

While men felt more of a sense of loss from lack of employment or reduced wages, women learned to be creative in managing the home. Deflation had lowered

CHILDHOOD IN THE UNITED STATES: 1930-1950

I tried to kill a streetcar by overturning it.

Pin Ford and I were hiding under a purple beech tree on the lawn of the Presbyterian seminary on Penn Avenue.

Through the beech's low dense branches she and I could make out Penn Avenue's streetcar lanes. It was midafternoon. Now a streetcar was coming toward us. We had been waiting. We had just stuck a stone in the streetcar track. This one seemed like a stone big enough to throw it over. Would the streetcar go over? Did we hope it would go over? We spotted its jiggling trolley stick first, high above the roofs of a cobblestone, and its lone simple eye. I pressed a thumb and finger between ribs on both sides of my breastbone, to try to calm myself. . .

The streetcar hit the stone audibly and rose like a beached whale. Its big orange body faltered in the air, heaved toward the lane of cars beside it, trembled, and finally fell down on its track and broke the stone. And went on, bumping again only slightly when the rear wheel went over it. Pin Ford and I lay low. – Annie Dillard. (1987). *An American childhood* (pp. 105-106). New York: Harper & Row

AN AMERICAN CHILDHOOD

It was your whole body that knew those sidewalks and streets. Your bones ached with them; you tasted their hot dust in your bleeding lip; their gravel worked into your palms and knees and stayed, blue under the new skin that grew over it.

You rode your bike across Penn Avenue with the light: a lane of asphalt, a sunken streetcar track just the width of a thin bike wheel, a few feet of brown cobblestones, another streetcar track, more cobblestones or some cement, more tracks, and another strip of asphalt. The old cobblestones were pale humpy ovals like loaves. When you rode your bike over them, you vibrated all over. A particularly long humpy cobblestone could knock you down in a twinkling if it caught your bike's front wheel. So could the streetcar's tracks, and they often did; your handlebars twisted in your hands and threw you like a wrestler. So you had to pay attention, alas, and could not simply coast along over cobblestones, blissfully vibrating all over. Now the city was replacing all the cobblestones, block by block. The cobblestones had come from Pittsburgh's riverbeds. In the nineteenth century, children had earned pennies by dragging them up from the water and selling them to paving contractors. They had been a great and late improvement on mud. – Annie Dillard. (1987). *An American childhood* (pp. 103-104). New York: Harper & Row.

the cost of food; nevertheless, mothers had to learn to stretch meat for meals or substitute inexpensive foods for items purchased in more affluent years. Clothing purchases and telephone use dropped sharply. Women did their own housework, sewed clothes at home and canned fruits and vegetables. Installment payments were used by some to maintain their standard of living.

Many women entered the labor market to supplement the family income. In some situations, there was resentment that women were taking jobs away from men. States passed laws prohibiting married women from employment. In the field of education, discrimination was frequently applied against the hiring of married women. Women were able to get clerical and sales jobs; however, they were paid lower wages than men. Although women played a major role in maintaining the family financially, their employment was concentrated in low-paying jobs with no opportunity for advancement.

Families made significant sacrifices of material goods, movies became a luxury for many, but the family automobile remained for limited outings. Family recreation, however, was one area of family life that was expanded during the 1930s. The federal government financed funds for the Civilian Conservation Corps (CCC) to build 20,000 construction projects that included stadiums, community centers and wading pools. Recreation leaders were trained and employed to expand existing recreation programs. The radio, outdoor community-sponsored activities, movies, magazines and books were other family leisure resources. Recreation continued to be viewed as a means for children to learn their place in society and to live a constructive life (Reynolds, 1976).

Conditions of Childhood

During the depression and war years, there was continuing concern for the plight of children, particularly children who were poor or handicapped. Federal efforts to improve conditions for children led to improvements in services provided for them and their families. New and expanded programs reflected the economic conditions of the period, as well as the displacement that resulted from a nation organized to fight a major war. In spite of advances in information and services, particularly in health care, children of the poor continued to lag in receiving the benefits available to the population as a whole.

Improvements in Health Care and Services. The major advance in health care for children during this period was in the reduction of communicable disease. In the mid-1930s, the U.S. Public Health Survey of households in urban and rural communities found that 51 percent of all deaths of children were due to infections, parasitic disease, pneumonia, diarrhea and enteritis. The cause of the deaths was found to be due to lack of medical care or delay in seeking medical aid. In 1938, the Children's Bureau held the Conference on Better Care for Mothers and Babies which reported impairment of health was still widespread among mothers and children. Although the medical field had the knowledge available to prevent maternal and infant deaths, the needed services were not reaching many populations, particularly the poor, and those living in rural areas.

Another cause of poor health during the Great Depression was malnutrition among poor children. In 1932, the Health Department in New York City reported that 20 percent of the school children examined were suffering from malnutrition. As the economic crisis deepened, medical care for children decreased and undernutrition increased. In spite of many federal relief efforts, child health was neglected (Public Health Service, 1976).

Social Security Act of 1935. In 1934, the Children's Bureau proposed a broad program to meet the health and social needs of the nation's children. The following year, the Social Security Act was signed into law. It enabled a federal-state partnership to provide medical care for crippled children. Provisions were also included for the health of mothers and children, strengthened public child welfare services, protection and care of homeless, dependent and neglected children and children in danger of becoming delinquent. Each state was to define the crippling conditions it would attempt to treat: orthopedic conditions, conditions requiring plastic surgery, operable eye conditions, rheumatic fever and eye diseases (Public Health Service, 1976).

The Social Security Act also provided old-age pensions and, later, payments to surviving dependents, including wives and children. Another provision was for unemployment insurance funded through a federal tax paid by the employer.

RURAL CHILDBIRTH

When a woman became pregnant, she usually had the support of her family and that of the community. In towns and cities, a doctor could easily be summoned to help in the delivery—if there was money to pay the doctor. Many physicians tended the poor, knowing that they would never receive any pay. Improved roads and the use of automobiles enabled doctors to cover more territory as well as permitting rural people to travel to town. Midwives, often called granny women, delivered many rural children. Few had any education or formal training, but most were savvy in special ways about delivery. They apprenticed themselves to other midwives, and the methods were traditional. As modern medicine introduced professionalism, granny women became rare. In some cases, midwives also prescribed potions that would induce abortion, but most women chose to bear their children. Although midwives had high status among the poor people of a community, many of the wealthy, including doctors, regarded them as nuisances. Once, a midwife, realizing that the delivery had become complicated, arrived at a small-town doctor's house after midnight to ask for help. She knocked for a quarter of an hour, and the doctor finally opened the door, cursed her, dallied about, and arrived after the infant had been born. Even in the 1950s midwives served poor blacks and whites who could not afford doctors. – Pete Daniel. (1986). *Standing at the crossroads* (pp. 85-86). New York: Hill & Wang.

BLACK BOY

Hunger stole upon me so slowly that at first I was not aware of what hunger really meant. Hunger had always been more or less at my elbow when I played, but now I began to wake up at night to find hunger standing at my bedside staring at me gauntly. The hunger I had known before this had been no grim, hostile stranger; it had been a normal hunger that had made me beg constantly for bread, and when I ate a crust or two I was satisfied. But this new hunger baffled me, scared me, made me angry and insistent. Whenever I begged for food now my mother would pour me a cup of tea which would still the clamor in my stomach for a moment or two; but a little later I would feel hunger nudging my ribs, twisting my empty guts until they ached. I would grow dizzy and my vision would dim. I became less active in my play, and for the first time in my life I had to pause and think of what was happening to me. – Richard Wright. (1937). *Black boy* (p. 13). New York: Harper & Brothers.

Benefits varied from state to state, and the limitation of unemployment insurance was that it failed to protect the chronically unemployed (Henretta et al., 1987).

Medical Care at Military Bases During WW II. As the country mobilized for World War II, a new need for health care arose at military bases. Because many wives followed their husbands who were being trained for compulsory military service, military establishments faced large numbers of wives seeking maternity care. The 1943 Congress, in response to this crisis, appropriated funds to initiate a new service, Emerging Maternity and Infant Care (EMIC), through the Children's Bureau that would provide medical care for wives and children of servicemen. The program was a cooperative effort that included the American Red Cross, Army and Navy relief societies and other public and private agencies. The program not only supported families during the war years of the 1940s, but led to the establishment of minimum standards for hospitals, maternity and newborn care. It also effected a significant drop in the national infant mortality rate (Public Health Service, 1976).

Foster Care. During WW II, the decrease in numbers of children needing foster care can be attributed to servicemen's dependency allowances, the increase of mothers employed in the defense effort and their ability to support themselves and their children, and the Lanham Act that expanded day care for children of working mothers. In contrast to the economic poverty caused by the Great Depression, World War II had some benefits for poor children. The reduction in children needing foster care was unfortunately short lived, and beginning in the mid-1940s, foster care rolls once again began to increase (Datta, 1976).

Conditions for Minority Children

The years of depression and war affected minority families in unique ways. Some groups were adversely affected; others received long overdue attention.

The problems of Native Americans and the extent of their poverty were a focus of concern during the 1930s. Native Americans had owned 138 million acres of land in the late 1880s but, by 1934, westward expansion, broken treaties and other events resulted in less than two-fifths of the original amount left, mostly in desert areas. The average Native American income totaled 48 dollars, and the unemployment rate was three times the national average. The federal government changed its policy of trying to integrate Native Americans into American society and began to focus attention on preserving Indian languages, arts, and their tribal heritage and history. More self-government was promoted through the Indian Reorganization Act of 1934, but little progress was made in solving Native American economic problems.

Black Americans were not as affected by the economic crisis as some populations because they were already poor when the economic downturn occurred. More than 75 percent of the Black population lived in the South; the great majority were tenant farmers, farm hands and sharecroppers. Nevertheless, as many as 200,000 Black tenant farmers were displaced from farms during the depression years.

As a result of the economic conditions in the South, as well as the activities of southern conservatives and organizations such as the Klu Klux Klan against Blacks, large numbers left for the North in the 1930s. About 400,000 Blacks moved to northern cities where they encountered racial segregation, excessive rents, high unemployment and crowded living conditions. In March 1935, the frustrations experienced by Blacks resulted in a major race riot in Harlem.

Blacks sought to strengthen their position through labor organizations. Activism expanded with the outbreak of World War II as Black workers protested their exclusion from defense plants. President Roosevelt established a fair employment practices policy that prohibited discrimination in the employment of workers in defense industries or the government. As Blacks migrated to defense centers seeking employment, social tensions increased. A race riot in Detroit in 1943 left 34 people dead, and was followed by racial conflicts in 43 cities (Henretta et al., 1987).

Japanese Americans were put into an unfortunate situation during WW II. West Coast residents became afraid of a Japanese attack after Pearl Harbor. Reacting to their fears of Japanese spies, President Roosevelt approved a War Department plan to intern Japanese Americans in relocation camps during the war. Although more than two-thirds of the Japanese affected were native-born Americans of Japanese ancestry, approximately 112,000 people were relocated in remote areas in California, Arizona, Utah, Colorado, Wyoming, Idaho and Arkansas. They were given a few days to sell or dispose of their possessions and could take with them only what they could carry.

All ten camps were located in hot, dusty climates, and their primitive conditions made family life nearly impossible. Communal bathroom and dining facilities undermined morale even more. The lack of privacy was hardest to bear; only flimsy partitions separated the hastily built rooms. When one baby cried, babies cried up and down the barracks. Eight people lived in a room that measured only twenty-five by twenty feet. Small families might have strangers assigned to their room. Generational differences between the Issei, who had an average of fifty-five, and the Nisei, who averaged seventeen years old, added to the tensions. Everyone found boredom a major problem. (Henretta et al., 1987, p. 820)

Because Japanese Americans had been important in agriculture, a labor shortage in farming led the government to furlough farm workers. College students were allowed to leave to resume their studies; and young men also volunteered for military service in Europe (Wishon & Spangler, 1990).

Before evacuation, I was the only Japanese in the whole school for about two years. I had been going to that school since kindergarten. When the attack was made on Pearl Harbor the people, especially the boys, called me bad names. Even though the boys called me names, the girls tried to help me. When evacuation time came, someway I did not want to go, but I had to. I didn't want to leave even if the people called me names. I had two dogs named Mike and Kiltie. They were Scotties. I did not want to leave them, but everything else that I liked besides my parents was left behind.

When we left, I kept my eyes open to look at the city where I had always lived, and which I might never see again. Living with Japanese around is strange to me, for all I knew about were Americans. I do not want to go to Japan for all the money in the World because I like the United States. – Wanda Robertson. (1943). Developing world citizens in a Japanese relocation center. *Childhood Education, 20*, 66-71.

What of Hispanic families? Poorly educated and hampered by language difficulties, Hispanic populations were poorer than mainstream populations. The depression years were hard for them.

Migrant labor became a way of life for many Hispanic families, both American and Mexican citizens. Families in the Southwest followed the crops each year, moving to Michigan and other northern states in the summer and working in Texas, California and Florida during the winter months. Living conditions were primitive. Children worked alongside adults from dawn to dusk; babies were left unattended while the families worked in the fields. Children attended school infrequently and became school dropouts by the time they were teenagers. Many young men enlisted in the armed services during World War II. Efforts to improve conditions for migrant workers and provide better education for migrant children did not become a reality until after the end of the war. The problems of migrant workers, however, continue to handicap them economically and educationally. Mechanization of crop harvesting has increasingly limited opportunity for migrant employment each year since the 1940s.

Any morning between seven and eight o'clock on a day when the weather is suitable for field work the labor contractor may be seen in the communities of agricultural workers with his large produce truck, assembling his crew of field workers from among his own family, his relatives and his neighbors. Infants who cannot yet walk are taken along because there is no one at home to care for them. Little children six and seven years old go along to run errands in the fields and gradually learn to work. – Amber Arthun Warburton. (1944). Children who work. *Childhood Education 20,* 221-226.

CHILDHOOD EDUCATION: COPING WITH DEPRESSION AND WAR

Expansion of American Education

American education grew rapidly in the 1930s. In spite of lower birthrates during depression years, compulsory attendance laws and expansion of consolidated school districts contributed to the increase in school attendance. In 1930, secondary school enrollments numbered 4,812,000, increasing to 7,100,000 in 1940 (Cremin, 1988).

As school districts continued to consolidate, they developed the resources to provide improved programs. School buses that first appeared in the 1920s were used in increasing numbers to transport students from rural areas. Attention was given to vocational programs at the secondary school level for those students who would be unable to attend college and needed job preparation. Centralization was also reflected in the work of the state departments of education that sponsored conferences and institutes, as well as the publication of curricula and instructional materials to disseminate current information on pedagogy to school districts.

The federal government was also concerned with the problems of poor youth. Because the government was suspicious of educational leaders, it did not turn to the schools to assist with youth training and unemployment; rather, the Civilian Conservation Corps and National Youth Administration were the vehicles used to employ and train these youth. The CCC provided work on conservation projects for young men between the ages of 18 and 25. In addition to earning money for themselves and their families, they learned social skills and standards of hygiene. More important, libraries were established in the camps and educational programs were offered to the workers. According to Cremin (1988), by June 1937, 35,000 illiterate young men had been taught to read and write, more than 1,000 had earned high school diplomas and 39 had received college degrees. Vocational training had also been provided in such occupations as carpentry, woodworking, boilermaking and metalwork. In the later years of the program, an extensive guidance program was established to help the men plan personal and vocational goals.

Progress in Child Study

Expanding child study research centers broadened the research in child development between 1930 and the 1950s. Research efforts were supported and advanced with the establishment of the Laura Spelman Rockefeller Memorial, the Society for Research in Child Development in 1933 and the Institute for Child Study at the University of Maryland in 1947 (Weber, 1984).

During the 1930s, new directions were taken in child study. As a result of research techniques that included interviews, observation and statistical analysis, family influences on child development could be investigated. Research indicated correlations between the family's socioeconomic level and the child's growth and development. In other words, it was apparent that the family's status determined both the parents' methods of childrearing and the goals and expectations that they held for their children. Kurt Lewin at the Iowa Child Welfare Research Station used sociological research techniques within a field theory framework to determine how the total environment affected child development and behavior. His findings were that there was a dynamic influence between the child and interaction with the total environment (Grotberg, 1976).

In the 1940s, the research focus moved to the study of personality development. Freudian psychology was to have a strong influence on child study; as a result, the relationship between experience and personality development was studied with particular attention to the effects of deprivation and institutionalization on later development. Much of the intent of the research was to remove the adverse conditions that would negatively affect development. Maternal deprivation studies showed subsequent mental retardation in infants and young children. Deprivation could contribute also to failure to thrive and a high child mortality rate. The role of culture in child development was also investigated. Studies of American subcultures and other cultures provided information on how cultural experiences affected child development.

Information from research had a strong influence on childrearing and educational practices in the 1930s and 1940s, particularly in early childhood education. Developmental theories and child study research, initiated in the 1920s, continued to have an impact on education during an era of progressive influence. The work of Gesell along with the maturation theory permeated educational practices, as well as Thorndike's stimulus-response theory, measurement of intelligence and the widespread use of testing in the schools.

Gesell's work in establishing developmental norms and the normative view of development had a pervasive influence on child study investigation and educational practice. The view that development must precede acquisition of skills, and readiness for learning rested upon developmental maturation, guided the planning for curriculum and instruction, not only in the early years of schooling, but in later childhood education as well.

Thorndike had his own understanding of the concept of readiness. His laws of learning were based on the connections established between the child's experiences and the external responses to the child's behaviors. Readiness for learning was established through positive attitudes developed as a result of satisfactory experiences. Through the modification of the child's responses, the laws of learning were meant to govern educational practice (Weber, 1984).

The Spreading Use of Standardized Tests

Thorndike also believed in the concept of a fixed intelligence. He built upon the work of Binet and Simon in France and L.M. Terman at Stanford University in the establishment of an intelligence quotient or IQ. Thorndike contributed to the expansion of the testing movement by adapting the measurement scale to measure achievement in arithmetic, spelling, reading and language ability.

The testing movement's influence began in the 1920s and expanded in the 1930s. It served as a major factor in the standardization of the schools as achievement tests were used for measuring achievement, grouping students and developing a standardized curriculum. Research was conducted on what children should and could learn and at what level. Homogeneous grouping based on achievement test results was intended to make both teaching and learning more effective (Snyder, 1972).

Although the goal of testing was to determine appropriate instructional strategies for students at a given time, it also had negative results. Tests for grouping children also came to be used as a tool to classify them. IQ tests and achievement test results were also used to place students into programs that could deny them access to a college track curriculum at the secondary level. Disagreement over the use of tests and misuse of their results led to sharp divisions among educators during the 1930s and 1940s which continue to plague American schools and educators in the 1990s.

Progressive Education

The influence of progressive educators in reforming schools in the 1920s was more widespread in the decades of the 1930s and 1940s. Progressive teaching methods had been adopted by significant numbers of schools and teachers at different levels of implementation. Moreover, the progressive movement had extended beyond the United States to Europe, the British Commonwealth and parts of Asia and South America after books by Dewey and Kilpatrick had been translated into other languages.

After WW II, progressive education had become generally accepted as the American model of education. Indeed, the accomplishments of the movement in the decades of implementation and expansion were impressive.

1. There was a steady extension of educational opportunity, downward as well as upward. A greater percentage of the population continued into the high schools, while kindergartens and nursery schools also flourished as the number of working women rose.
2. Numbers of school systems shifted from an eight-year elementary school followed by a four-year high school to a six-year elementary school followed by a three-year junior high school and then a three-year senior high school, partly to give greater attention to the special requirements of pubescent children.
3. There was a continuing expansion and reorganization of the curriculum at all levels, and frequently in directions advocated by the progressives. In the secondary schools in particular there were vastly extended opportunities for work in trades, agriculture, home economics, physical education, and the arts.
4. Along with the proliferation and reorganization of the formal curriculum, there came a concomitant expansion of extracurricular–or as the progressives called them to emphasize their integral part in the school program, "cocurricular"–activities. The informal student clubs and activities that had been radical innovations at the turn of the century became established features of the American school.
5. There was infinitely more variation and flexibility in the grouping of students, most commonly on the basis of intelligence and achievement tests. In addition, as districts consolidated and schools became larger, guidance programs developed in an effort to take account of the varying needs and concerns of individual youngsters.
6. The character of the classroom changed markedly, especially at the elementary level, as projects began to compete with recitations as standard pedagogical procedure. Students and teachers alike tended to be more active, more mobile, and more informal in their relationships with one another.
7. The materials of instruction changed dramatically as those who prepared them sought to incorporate the latest research on learning and child development. Textbooks became more colorful and attractive, and supplementary devices like flash cards, workbooks, simulated newspapers, slides, filmstrips, and phonograph records were used in growing numbers. In addition there were innumerable attempts to employ indigenous materials, ranging from local flora and fauna to locally manufactured products, in the course of instruction.
8. School architecture was modified to take account of the new developments, thereby lending them a measure of permanence. Assembly rooms, gymnasiums, swimming pools, playgrounds, athletic fields, laboratories, shops, kitchens, cafeterias, and infirmaries; miniature tables and chairs; movable furniture and partitions, improved lighting and ventilation–all testified eloquently to the changing programs and commitment of the school.
9. Teachers were better educated; and by virtue of state certification requirements, their programs of preparation–both preservice and inservice–increasingly included professional courses that tended to reflect one or another of the versions of progressive education.
10. Finally, administrative relationships changed, if somewhat paradoxically. As schools and school systems became larger, bureaucracy increased; school administration became a separate professional function rather than a responsibility of the senior teachers. At the same time teachers were allowed a somewhat greater role in the determination of curriculum, while parents exercised a measure of influence through parent and parent-teacher associations. At few points did school boards or administrators relinquish important powers; nonetheless, there was perceptible growth of parent and teacher participation in policymaking. (Cremin, 1961, pp. 306-308)

Experimentation with progressive methods had extended also to higher education after World War II. There was examination of the merits of a liberal education and how to humanize and integrate knowledge through instruction. More than 100 reform efforts had been initiated in higher education curriculum (Cremin, 1961).

Reappraisal of Progressive Education

There are two groups who make it difficult for the inquiring individual to get an adequate picture of progressive education. The more dangerous group consists of those who call themselves progressive who attempt to "put over" progressive education in the form of an activity program. They take inordinately rapid strides; they countenance, and perhaps even boast of, an utter lack of discipline; and they disregard the skills and controls so necessary for effective self-direction. The other group consists of those reactionary critics who use such extreme practices as the target for their witticisms and damaging statements. This is characteristic of the prevailing tendency to establish the extreme as the norm—always unfair and confusing. The great majority of really progressive developments have crept in and have been accepted as part of a slower growth process which moves in closer harmony with the nature of man. The critics conscientiously avoid mention of these developments, and the pseudo-progressives reject the slower but psychologically sound methods which are essential for growth. – Alice V. Keliher. (1935). What about progressive education? *Childhood Education, 11,* 243.

Not all schools followed Dewey's progressive ideas. The influence of the testing movement had led many schools to implement curriculum and teaching methods that were compatible with achievement and intelligence test results. The two schools of thought on what was the best education for students gained advocates and followers in the decades of educational improvement in the 1930s and 1940s.

Progressive schools were colorful and were designed and arranged to be conducive to creativeness. Model schools such as Lincoln School (established through Teachers College), Porter School (a model rural school in Missouri) and the public schools in Winnetka, Illinois, had all paved the way for progressive education in the various settings (Cremin, 1961).

Standardization of education through the use of advances in science and

RADIO: PIED PIPER OR EDUCATOR?
Few topics of interest to parents and teachers of young children have aroused so much controversy as the question whether children's radio programs are an instrument of exploitation, a form of harmless entertainment, or a means for the development of a greater appreciation of life. Judging by those expressions of opinion which are found in published sources, the majority of commentators incline to the view that radio has at least failed to play a significantly beneficial part in the education of children. Even commercial observers have deplored what they regard as the poor business sense exhibited by sponsors of allegedly objectionable children's programs. "Into the ears of defenseless children," asserts Don Gridley in Printer's Ink for April 9, 1936, "there were poured the moans and shrieks of dying men and women; the sharp, menacing rattle of the machine guns; the language of the gutter and all the other ingredients of the hair-raising thriller." – John J. DeBoer. (1939). Radio: Pied piper or educator? *Childhood Education 16,* 74-79.

technology was seen by those in the testing movement to be the route of school improvement. Research to determine what all children should learn and at what grade level led to attempts to revitalize the curriculum through careful design and selection of curriculum.

While both movements had their supporters, both created concern and critics. The schools' use of standardized test results for grouping, placement and development of a standardized curriculum generated a great deal of concern, particularly the misuse of testing results for placing and teaching students.

Despite apparent successes in the progressive movement after WW II, a crisis over progressive methods was beginning to appear in the press. Much earlier, Professor George S. Counts had expressed concern that progressive schools were not bearing the responsibility to build a better social order. He anticipated the disaster of the depression years and challenged the schools to address the relationship between schools and society (Cremin, 1961).

In the 1940s, although progressive methods such as group work, field trips and project activities were common teaching practices, most teachers used teacher-directed instructional approaches. In addition, some progressive strategies had been taken out of the context within which they had originally been intended to be taught. In *Experience and Education* (1938), Dewey discussed some of his disappointments with how his theory was implemented in progressive methods (Cremin, 1988). The use of activities to make subject matter more concrete, for example, now rapidly became a substitute for academic knowledge. In another major shift, the original intent to give students an appreciation of industrial society now became the path for vocational education. The push for vocational education was to become the focus of the most critical attacks on progressive education.

The Vocational Education Division of the United States Office of Education studied the problems of high school students in 1944. Because the study revealed that many high school students were served neither by college preparatory nor vocational programs, a series of conferences was called to address the failure of secondary schools to address the life-adjustment problems of a majority of their students. A Commission of Life Adjustment Education for Youth was created to translate the thesis of progressive education into programs that would provide a universal secondary education to prepare all youth to live in a society that must utilize scientific discoveries (Cremin, 1961).

The life adjustment curriculum came under early and strong attack by critics of the progressive movement; moreover, the progressive movement in general came under broad attack. Following World War II, pressures of money, the threat of communism, teacher shortages and booming enrollments placed schools in a crisis situation. Schools were criticized for misplacing priorities in education, coddling students and not preparing them for the manpower needs of the rapidly changing and expanding industrial economy. Critics made sweeping indictments of public education that were counterattacked by the progressives.

When the Russians launched the first space satellite in 1957, it served as a catalyst for educational reform and the end of the progressive movement. Progressive education quickly collapsed, partly because it had not continued to adapt to the changes in American society. Economic changes, continued advances in mass media and extension of industry-sponsored educational programs had moved into new approaches to instruction and the progressive movement had not kept pace (Cremin, 1961). The 1950s marked a period of vast changes in education as the country and American education sought to meet the new challenges of the Cold War era.

Minority Education

If public schools, in general, were hampered by the years of depression poverty, followed by shortages resulting from the war effort, education of minorities was hit even harder. A reality for many decades, resources for schools for White students contrasted sharply with monies available for minority schools; but the 1930s and 1940s saw even deeper differences in funding as financial cuts were made.

Schools for Black Children. Black students continued to be educated in separate schools. Although the concept of separate but equal schools had never been a reality, Black families in the South found themselves having to fund schooling for their children even before the depression years. In the 1920s, public school funds for Black children were regularly diverted to White schools. Black taxpayers found it necessary to raise money for schools for Black children in addition to paying school taxes in the community.

Southern Whites had little motivation to provide schooling for Blacks. In an agrarian rural society, Black children were seen primarily as a source of labor. Education of Black children was regarded as a distraction for their potential cheap labor source by White landowners. Public school funds were unavailable not only for construction of school buildings for Black students, but also for other services related to schooling. Transportation provided for White students was withheld from Black children, forcing them to walk to school. School maintenance, supplies and teaching materials had to be provided by parents and teachers.

When the Black migration from the South resulted in a loss of Black laborers after 1910, efforts were made to establish an improved Black school system to stop the exodus. Black citizens engaged in grassroots efforts to build better schools for their children. Moreover, philanthropic contributions, including the Negro Rural School Fund and, more significantly, the Julius Rosenwald Fund, also made it possible for the construction of rural Black schools in southern states. Because Rosenwald funds required local matching resources, Black parents and community leaders had to raise money locally and volunteer their time to supplement the financial support available to them. A frequent method was for children to solicit small amounts of cash in a community drive. Another resource was Black landowners who donated lumber for the school cut from trees on their own property. Parents also volunteered to construct school buildings.

These efforts were very successful. By 1927, the Julius Rosenwald Fund had assisted in the construction of 3,769 school buildings in 14 southern states (Anderson, 1988). At the same time, White landowners also began to return a larger share of public tax funds for rural Black schools because of their growing concern over the continued migration North of Black tenants, laborers, sharecroppers and domestic servants.

As the Great Depression evolved in the 1930s, Blacks were already among the nation's poorest and found it impossible to continue raising the money to support schools for their children. School construction, maintenance and funds for school operation declined, both from lack of continued funding of the Rosenwald school program and economic destitution at the local level. Nevertheless, efforts for a Black school system in the South had resulted in a more developed elementary school system for the children. School enrollment and attendance increased dramatically. By 1935, enough elementary schools had been built to enroll the majority of Black children. By 1940, 66 percent of Black children and 65 percent of White children in southern states between the ages of 5 and 9 were enrolled in school (Anderson, 1988). The Black schools were grossly inadequate when compared to schools for White students, but opportunities for schooling were now available where, previously, none existed.

Schools for Japanese Children in Internment Camps. In March 1942, three months after the United States entered World War II, President Roosevelt established the War Relocation Authority that ordered the relocation of people of Japanese ancestry who lived on the west coast to 10 internment camps. Of the approximately 112,000 Japanese Americans relocated, more than 30,000 were children under the age of 15.

Although each camp had established a school system by the summer of 1942, the hastily constructed barracks and other buildings had not included plans for schooling. As a result, the schools opened in barracks buildings with no school furniture, materials, supplies or books. Few qualified teachers were available initially; therefore, former Japanese-American college students were used as assistant teachers who worked under the supervision of Caucasian teachers. Eventually the needed supplies, equipment and furniture were made available and instruction for the students improved (Wishon & Spangler, 1990).

Schools for Native American Children. Little attention was given to the plight of Native American children prior to the end of World War II. Although the National Council of American Indians lobbied for better conditions during the 1940s, little changed until the Civil Rights movement in the 1960s and 1970s. Young Native American children attended schools on the reservation for the first years of schooling, a system that had been established prior to the turn of the century. They then attended boarding schools off of the reservation for the remainder of elementary and secondary education. The adjustment to a different culture away from the security of home was difficult for most students. A teacher, Mrs. Chumbley Zeir, who wrote about the curriculum being used at one Indian school, provided information about the educational practices used with Native American students.

We have about one hundred and forty pupils in our school and have five teachers. The children spend one year in the kindergarten; after they have finished the first grade, they go away, usually to non-reservation schools. The children come from non-English speaking homes and are named when they enter school. The children are brought to school in the fall and live in dormitories. During the first few months of school the smaller children are prone to run away from school. (Zeir, 1933, P. 80)

At the end of World War II, the nation focused on a return to a postwar economy and culture. The practice of separate or unequal schools for Blacks, Hispanics, Native Americans and Asian Americans continued, but would shortly be challenged. The economic opportunities and experiences of military service in the war had altered the expectations of minority groups for education, employment and full recognition as members of the community. Criticism of discrimination because of race, religion or other factors gained national attention. President Truman's Commission on Higher Education proposed that the nation's economy required that educational opportunity be broadened to include large numbers of Americans who were currently denied higher education because of race, class, gender and national origin. In 1946, 17 states still required separate schools for Whites and Blacks by law; moreover, separate schools for Blacks were operating in other states contrary to state law.

The Committee on Civil Rights reported patterns of discrimination of long standing against Jews, Roman Catholics, Blacks, Native Americans and persons of Hispanic, Filipino and Asian descent. The report described discrimination in employment, housing, health and education and disclosed that Blacks in the 17 states with legally separate schools were particularly disadvantaged in the quality of education available. The difference in educational attainment between Blacks and Whites, however, was also significant in the North and West. In 1948, President

Truman called for legislation prohibiting lynching, outlawing the poll tax and establishing commissions for fair employment practices and civil rights to protect minorities against discrimination. Although Congress did not immediately respond, the Brown court decision in 1954 and 1955 paved the way for the end of separate systems of schooling and other forms of discrimination in the 1950s and 1960s.

EARLY CHILDHOOD EDUCATION: PROVIDING EDUCATION AND CARE DURING DEPRESSION AND WAR

The decades of depression and war had significant effects on the field of early childhood education. Kindergartens that had experienced constant growth within public school systems were faced with budget cuts when public school systems felt the economic consequences of the Great Depression. Conversely, the nursery school and child care movement experienced tremendous growth as federal government efforts to provide work included WPA nursery schools to make possible employment for teachers and care for children of working mothers. Similar funding during World War II enabled parents to work in industries that were part of the war effort.

Educational trends of the period impacted curriculum development in early childhood programs, but at the same time fostered controversy and conflict. The decades of the 1930s and 1940s were a period of growth and uncertainty in teaching methods as teachers in various kinds of settings attempted to sort out the implications for practice of various psychological theories of growth and development, learning and measurement and testing.

Influence of Research in Child Growth and Development on Early Childhood Education

Arnold Gesell's Maturational Theory. The child study movement continued to have an influence on early childhood education. Arnold Gesell's ongoing work in child development was based on his theory of maturation and the natural unfolding of the child. Early childhood specialists found Gesell's ideas of the relationship between development and learning sensible in terms of planning curriculum for young children. The concepts of maturation and readiness were widely discussed in textbooks of the period for kindergarten teachers.

Although Gesell exerted a strong influence, he was not without critics. The description of the average child and curriculum constructed according to normative data generated concern because of the lack of attention to individual differences. In addition, his use of the children of students and professors at Yale to establish norms was criticized because the influence of environment on children from diverse populations was not considered. In spite of these concerns, Gesell's impact on early childhood curriculum continued for several decades.

Behaviorism and the Measurement Movement. Thorndike's study of the laws of learning and ideas of connectionism proposed that the young child was modifiable. Stimulus and response could be used by the teacher to form appropriate behaviors. Thorndike believed that kindergarten was the place for good habits to be formed in young children, specifically habits of obedience, cheerfulness, self-help, courage and modesty.

Patty Smith Hill demonstrated Thorndike's influence while teaching at Teachers College, Columbia University. She and her students and classroom teachers used an inventory of behaviors or habits that was later followed by a "conduct curriculum" that included the need to measure results of learning (Snyder, 1972). Hill not only believed that early childhood included the primary years, but also extended downward from kindergarten. As an early supporter of nursery education, she included the conduct curriculum for nursery school experiences. Although Hill's reconstructed kindergarten curriculum and curriculum for 1st grade reflected Thorndike's views, she was also influenced by John Dewey. Her writing and work reflected both elements of progressive education, but the inclusion of lists of objectives and suggestions for measurement reflected a need for more specificity in children's learning (Weber, 1984).

Dewey's Progressivism in Early Childhood Education. Dewey's beliefs and suggestions for progressive education perhaps had their greatest influence in the years between 1930 and the late 1950s. Application of his principles of purposeful activities in the learning process and the classroom as a small community extended into kindergarten curriculum practices in the 1930s and 1940s. Dewey shared an understanding of how the child learns with Piaget's beliefs that became more familiar in the 1950s. He, too, proposed that the child was an actively learning being. Interaction with materials in the environment fostered learning by doing. Interaction also meant involvement with the world of ideas. Learning must be meaningful and include problem-solving. In *Experience and Education* (1936), Dewey discussed the importance of the quality of experience:

> Everything depends on the quality of the experience which is had. The quality of any experience has two aspects. There is an immediate aspect of agreeableness or disagreeableness, and there is its influence on later experiences. The effect of an experience is not born on its face. It sets a problem to the educator. It is his business to arrange for the kind of experiences which, while they do not repel the student, but rather engage his activities are, nevertheless, more than immediately enjoyable since they promote having desirable future experiences. (p. 16)

At the University of Chicago, Alice Temple had a primary role in translating Dewey's influence into early childhood education. She first came into contact with Dewey through her experiences as a teacher and principal at the Chicago Free Kindergarten Association where she participated in Anna Bryan's design of new kindergarten procedures to replace Froebelian methods. In 1929, Temple was chairman of the kindergarten-primary department at the University of Chicago; and, although Dewey had left for Columbia University, she continued his legacy that preschool and primary grades should be combined.

Teachers at the Laboratory School established by Dewey continued to teach following his educational convictions. From them, she was able to collect materials and activities that demonstrated his methods for kindergarten (Weber, 1984). Dewey's theories of learning were described in *Unified Kindergarten and First-Grade Teaching* (Parker & Temple, 1925) with their practical application in the physical environment, class organization, curriculum design and learning activities. The Parker and Temple text also showed the influence of the testing movement; nonetheless, the majority of information in the text was an advocacy of Dewey's emphasis on child-centered instruction (Snyder, 1972). This and other publications guided kindergarten and primary teachers in their teaching methods in the decades to follow.

Psychoanalysis in Early Childhood Education. While kindergartens of the 1930s and 1940s reflected Dewey's principles of education and Thorndike's habit formation resulting from connectionism, Freudian psychology was also affecting the direction of the nursery school movement. Norms established for 4-year-olds by Gesell and related to motor development, personal habits and adaptive behavior were included in nursery school procedures, as was habit formation through techniques of conditioning behavior. Nevertheless, sound emotional development based on aspects of psychoanalytical thinking had its own influence on preschool or nursery education in both the United States and England.

Within Freud's stages of personality development, the period of early childhood was significant. Freud spent little time working with young children; however, emotional factors as an important aspect of child development became a concept in nursery education. The child's sense of security, the dangers of too rigid an emphasis on habit-building and the importance of expressive play influenced nursery school curriculum development and, to a lesser extent, the kindergarten.

Lawrence Frank and Child Care. If Patty Smith Hill and Alice Temple were primary interpreters and translators of progressive theory into practice in early childhood education, Lawrence Frank modified Freud's theory of personality development for child care and nursery education. Through the Laura Spelman Rockefeller Memorial, Frank was able to study the child's affective development and how early childhood was important in providing the best climate for the child's emotional growth.

Frank's goal through the child study institutes was to learn about the child's development and how the studies could explain the importance of the child's struggles in emotional development. The information gained from his studies could be used to improve nursery education and care of preschool children. Frank disseminated his views as a neo-Freudian through lectures and articles. He discussed emotional development in terms of the child's needs and the process of socialization. He proposed that, if children were given affection and were accepted as having individual temperaments in the early years, they could become well-adjusted adults. Frank believed that individual children had different emotional needs. Child caregivers and nursery school teachers needed to address children's emotional problems in early childhood to include sibling rivalry, fears, controlling emotions and accepting authority. Patience and reassurance by parents and teachers would help promote healthy personalities in young children.

In addition to working with Freud's ideas on personality development, Frank also was an early advocate of the theories of Jean Piaget and of the role of play. For Frank, the study and observation of play was a vehicle for understanding the child's development and social adjustment (Weber, 1984).

Overlapping Movements in Early Childhood Education

The late 19th century and early decades of the 20th century were the seminal years for the establishment of the field of early childhood education. Kindergarten, day nurseries and nursery schools were described as different movements in the 19th century. In reality, as these various programs were implemented, they were commingled and influenced each other. A broad spectrum of the population was involved in the education and care of young children during this period, representing churches, philanthropic agencies, parent groups, public school personnel, college and university researchers and teachers. Each of these groups serving young children was influenced by resources and methods being developed by the other groups with whom they had contact.

The philanthropic, religious and club or organizational groups, concerned with immigrant, orphaned or neglected children, became known as the "child savers" (Cooper, 1893; Cremin, 1988). They sought to save these poor children through education, parent training, playground development, day care and recreational programs. Accordingly, kindergartens, nursery schools, day nurseries, parent training and visitation were all implemented by churches, settlement houses and women's clubs. These groups were influenced by Froebelian kindergartens, the Macmillan Nursery school movement, the child study work at universities and philanthropic research organizations such as the Laura Spelman Rockefeller Memorial. Frequently these programs operated side-by-side in a cooperative manner in a single building (Cremin, 1988).

The concept of providing child care for working parents was a motivation for some child savers from the middle of the 19th century. The separation of education from care was difficult to delineate in many settings in the early years of program development because services and programs overlapped. Children attending a kindergarten might go to a day nursery in a settlement house in the afternoons. Younger children might accompany a sibling to a nursery school or kindergarten program. A kindergarten might in reality provide all-day care as an extension of the educational program.

Neugebauer (1990) listed 50 of the nation's oldest child care programs that were established between 1835 and 1911. Some of the organizations providing continuous services from the year of organization to the present include the St. Vincent Home, Philadelphia (1854); Golden Gate Kindergarten Association, San Francisco (1879); Bethlehem Day Nursery, New York (1885); Salvation Army Day Care Center, Philadelphia (1892); Jenkintown Day Nursery, Jenkintown, Pennsylvania (1903); and Childhaven, Seattle (1909).

By the advent of the 1930s, the progressive movement and child study movement were affecting the field of early childhood education in all its many programs and settings. Nursery schools reflected the work of laboratory schools and child study research. At the same time, public schools concurrently reflected the establishment of developmental norms, evaluation of learning through achievement testing and pedagogical practices following Dewey's democratic principles.

Philanthropic schools were declining in number as social services and federal funding for poor families allowed more low-income mothers to remain in the home to care for their children. Economic conditions in the 1930s and 1940s, to the contrary, resulted in expansion of early childhood education, especially in the area of child care, to alleviate parental need for a place for their children as they worked during depression and war.

Decline of Kindergartens. As a result of cuts in public school budgets during the depression, kindergarten classrooms were discontinued or combined with large enrollments. A low priority was given to kindergartens in contrast to primary classrooms. Although financial conditions were undoubtedly a major cause for the decline, other forces also impacted on the loss of influence for the continued growth of kindergartens (Weber, 1969).

One cause for the loss of influence was the end of "child savers" in kindergarten programs. During the peak years of growth in the kindergarten movement before 1930, there was lively interest in kindergartens on the part of nonprofessionals. Lay people from various walks of life became interested in the kindergarten and its potential for alleviating the hardships of poor children and their families. Kindergartens in nonpublic school settings were staffed by teachers from many backgrounds; however, philanthropic kindergartens decreased as public school programs expanded. Simultaneously, professional training for kindergarten teachers at colleges and universities and limited manuscripts about kindergarten in professional journals further divided professionals from the community.

With the loss of broad public interest and support, the kindergarten was more frequently perceived as a downward extension of the public school. The kindergarten curriculum had become rigid; further, kindergarten teachers and leaders were communicating with each other instead of with the nursery school and elementary grade teachers and administrators. Because of the lack of dialogue, kindergartens became the recipients of change instead of innovative leaders.

The decrease in the perceived importance of the kindergarten evoked an expansion in the influence of the elementary school on kindergarten curriculum. Kindergarten as preparation for 1st grade became the perception of primary teachers and school administrators. The maturation theory, concepts of school readiness, connectionism, habit formation and measurable learning all gradually modified kindergarten curriculum to conform to the expectations of elementary teachers and principals that children acquire "readiness" for 1st grade. Reading readiness, workbooks and testing in kindergarten vied with principles of child development in teaching practices. The kindergarten teacher struggled to resolve the conflict between active learning, learning centers with concrete materials, and project or theme studies with formalized instruction for preparation for academic learning. Then, as in future decades, practice probably reflected a range of teaching methods as teachers sought to determine which influences to accept and use in their classroom. Historical events in the 1950s that ended the progressive era would pave the way for renewed interest in early childhood education and new efforts to find the best way to facilitate learning in the early childhood years.

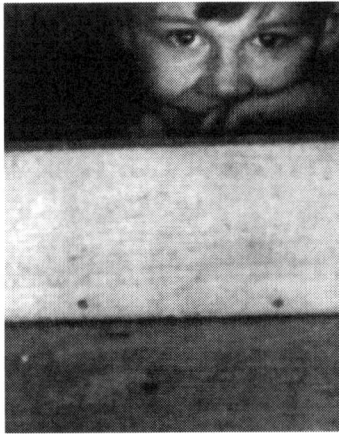

Expansion of Nursery Schools. Although the emergency triggered by the collapse of the stock market in 1929 lowered the priority for kindergartens in public school systems, it had the opposite effect on nursery schools. When the federal government took action to facilitate income for families through women entering the workforce, the provision of federally funded child care through nursery schools was the vehicle used to achieve their objective. This effort added to the number of nursery schools that had already been established during their rapid growth in the 1920s.

At this point, it is necessary to differentiate between nursery schools and day nurseries. Day nurseries had as their primary purpose to provide custodial care for children of the poor who were too young to attend kindergarten or primary school. They originated in homes, but were developed by private, philanthropic and religious institutions to serve the estimated 200,000 children under 5, in 1892, who were roaming the streets without supervision while their parents worked (Cremin, 1988). The day nurseries varied in quality, ranging from minimal care to efforts to provide an educational program for the children and in many cases, for other family members as well. Provisions for pensions for poor mothers with dependent children after 1918 affected day nurseries as they did philanthropic kindergartens. The possibility for mothers to receive assistance that allowed them to stay home,

plus the expansion of public school kindergartens that also served poor children, reduced the need for day nurseries.

Nursery schools were different. The nursery schools in England, established by Rachel and Margaret McMillan for poor children, were implemented in the United States as part of the child study movement. Their numbers grew with the support of the Laura Spelman Rockefeller Memorial for research in child development.

There were approximately 300 nursery schools in the 1930s. When the Federal Emergency Relief Administration determined the establishment of day care for children of poor and needy parents, the model of nursery schools with objectives for social, educational and physical development replaced custodial care of the earlier day nurseries (Cremin, 1988).

The Works Progress Administration, in 1935, included a Division in Education Projects that took responsibility for the nursery school program. WPA nursery schools took many forms. They continued in connection with colleges, universities and normal schools, were part of high school home economics departments and were implemented through local community agencies. In 1937, the WPA supported 1,472 nursery schools with an enrollment of 39,873 children. Lawrence Frank described the rapid implementation of these nursery schools:

> Within a remarkably short period of time, the emergency nursery schools and parent education programs were operating all over the country, involving the participation of many individuals and using the premises and facilities of various organizations to house the nursery schools and provide for parent meetings. Looking back, and seeing all the limitations and often exasperating delays, handicaps, and resistance to programs, we can say that, nevertheless, something of great significance was achieved. Through this emergency program, nursery schools which had been limited in numbers and were but slightly known by the public generally, became widely recognized and were generally accepted all over the country. . . . (Braun & Edwards, 1972, p. 160)

The end of the Great Depression came with the mobilization for war. Many WPA nursery schools continued under the Lanham Community Facilities Act, which funded child care facilities in communities affected by population shifts due to the war effort. While one major purpose of these nursery schools had been to provide work for unemployed teachers, Lanham Act Nursery Schools facilitated child care for working women. The purpose of nursery schools during World War II was again custodial care; nevertheless, the influences of the child study movement were mingled in with child care between 1941 and 1945. Lanham Act nursery schools were no longer funded after 1945 (Cremin, 1988). Mothers were expected to resume their responsibilities in the home during peacetime.

In reality, from the end of World War II to the present decade, the number of mothers working outside the home has risen steadily. Whether the federal government acknowledged the need for child care or not, it had become a necessity in the United States. In the absence of federal support, child care again evolved from private nonprofit and commercial sources.

ASSOCIATION FOR
CHILDHOOD EDUCATION INTERNATIONAL : 1930-1950

The two decades of the 1930s and 1940s were years of expansion in growth and influence for the organization, originally comprised mostly of people involved with the kindergarten movement. Through organizational growth, publications and annual conferences, the International Kindergarten Union served an ever-widening group of children, public and private school personnel, administrators and university groups.

An immediate source of expansion was the union of IKU with the National Council of Primary Education on February 4, 1931. The relationship between kindergarten and primary teachers had been developing since kindergartens became part of public schools. The early years of conflict between primary and kindergarten teachers had been ameliorated through working and planning together to teach their students. Textbooks and other publications espousing a unified approach to teaching between kindergarten and primary grades helped pave the way for the two organizations to come together. Nevertheless, it took time for members of IKU and the National Council of Primary Education to determine that it was in their best interest to join forces.

The National Council of Primary Education, organized in 1916, had experienced its own success in growth of membership and publication of helpful resources for primary teachers. For IKU members, the concept of serving age groups beyond the kindergarten had already become a reality with the evolution of the nursery school movement. When attention became focused on the needs of nursery school children and teachers, IKU members realized that their organization could have a broader purpose in serving educators. By 1926, active negotiations were under way between the two organizations. Many educators were members of both organizations, and there was communication both through individual correspondence and official reports on progress toward union (ACEI Archives).

At the 1930 annual meeting of IKU in Memphis, the Conferring Committee reported its support for unification with points that indicated an understanding that the field of early childhood education was bigger than separate movements. Smith (1942) reported three significant points from the report:

- The psychology of the child for the years from two to eight revealed common needs.
- Normal schools and colleges of education had unified kindergarten and primary teaching in kindergarten-primary courses and departments.
- A unified organization could bring greatly enlarged and more forceful influence to bear in promoting progressive nursery school, kindergarten, and primary work throughout the country. (p. 90)

In spite of the reluctance of some IKU members—particularly in giving up the name of the organization—the membership voted for the merger and renamed the organization the Association for Childhood Education (ACE). In 1931, at its annual meeting, the National Council of Primary Education accepted the action of IKU and voted to become members of the Association for Childhood Education (Smith, 1942).

While the membership of ACE represented a broader segment of the field of educators of young children, the National Association for Nursery Education (NANE) was organized for nursery educators in 1929 (Braun & Edwards, 1972). Many early childhood educators held membership in both organizations and close cooperation between the two lasted for many decades. In 1964, NANE became the National Association for the Education of Young Children (Weber, 1969). NAEYC has since become a major force in the field of early childhood education, especially through its significant work in day care issues. This focus on day care has been a factor in NAEYC's growth in recent years.

Depression Years

During the depression years of the 1930s, the Association for Childhood Education addressed the needs of teachers hired to teach in nursery schools sponsored by federal funding through the WPA. A major purpose of the WPA nursery school was to provide employment for teachers who were out of work as a result of the economic crisis. ACE tried to meet the needs of these teachers in conference topics and publications. *Childhood Education* was a major resource used to interpret and report the positions and issues of the day. The writings of leaders in the field such as Arnold Gesell, G. Stanley Hall, Patty Smith Hill, Alice Temple and William S. Gray were often published in this journal.

The loss of income for kindergarten teachers, resulting from reduced public school budgets, also affected ACE. Memberships, subscriptions to *Childhood Education* and sales of publications fell. In two reports to the Executive Board in 1933, Ross Barrett, Jr. and Peter Becker, Jr., ACE financial advisers, urged members of the board to be aware not only of the situation faced by schools with reduced appropriations, but also the need to produce publications that better reflect the needs of the membership and the field of early childhood education. In a report dated June 24, 1933, they stated:

> During the past year there has been a serious and widespread attack upon the fundamentals of early childhood education. This attack has taken the form of reduced educational appropriations, but what it actually means is:
> 1. The withdrawal of *any* educational opportunities for thousands of young children;
> 2. The *severe limitations* of educational opportunities for many other thousands of young children;
> 3. The elimination of all income of many teachers, through loss of their positions;
> 4. A substantial, and in some cases drastic, reduction in the income of those who still retain their positions;
> 5. The paring of allowances for equipment and supplies until, in some cases, they are no longer adequate for proper instruction. (Barrett & Becker, 1933, p. 1)

The advisers recommended that ACE take a greater interest in legislative and fiscal activities affecting the field of early childhood education and that publications be improved to reflect the concerns of teachers affected by the depression. In a second report in December, the advisers again urged the Association to be aware of reduced income and to modify publications to be more appealing and relevant for the current situation (Becker, 1933).

In 1937, ACE celebrated the centennial of the establishment of kindergartens in the United States. A bulletin, *The Kindergarten Centennial* 1837-1937 (The ACE Kindergarten Centennial Committee, 1937), was published as part of the celebration. The bulletin included the history of the kindergarten, particularly in the United States, and information on relevant publications and leaders in the kindergarten movement.

World War II and Postwar Years of the 1940s

The year 1942 marked the 50th anniversary of ACE. The anniversary conference was to be the last annual one until 1946 because of World War II restrictions. In 50 years, the organization had grown from 68 contributing members, two life members and nine branches to 2,957 contributing members, 114 life members and 508 branches with a combined membership of 34,000. The strength of the organization was in the branches. Through these groups and their work in local communities, ACE was influential and effective (Smith, 1942). In spite of ACE's overall growth since 1892, individual members dropped from 3,063 to 2,740 between 1942 and 1943 (Bain, 1967).

ACE was an active participant in the war effort. When severe travel restrictions resulted in a temporary halt to annual study conferences, well-attended community and regional conferences were held instead. Regional conferences reflected wartime topics, especially the needs of children during war years. Elections and other Association business were conducted by mail rather than through annual conferences.

In 1944, the Office of Defense Transportation issued a new ruling allowing conferences of no more than 254 participants; therefore, ACE was able to hold a restricted annual conference in Washington, D.C., that April. Participants not only were addressed by both Eleanor Roosevelt and Margaret Meade, but also were invited to the White House (Bain, 1967).

The war years and the second half of the decade following the war reflected the influence and service of the organization. Publications had grown in number and influence. During the war years, new publications were developed to meet wartime needs. Bain (1967) reported that, in 1944, 44,685 bulletins had been sold to child care centers, nursery groups, church school groups, defense councils, welfare groups and libraries in the United States, Australia, South Africa, India and England.

ACE's national prominence was also reflected in its work with other organizations and agencies. These groups included the Women's Joint Congressional Committee, American Council on Education Commission on Teacher Education, American Association of University Women, National Commission on Safety Education, Education Policies Commission and Council on Cooperation in Teacher Education. Joint projects resulted in publications to serve the needs of children. Perhaps the most important publication from such cooperative efforts resulted from the work of eight national organizations. Titled *The Nation and Its Children* (1945), the report was a statement of national policies affecting young children. More than 100,000 copies were distributed, including one presented to President Truman as a guide to the establishment of a national program to meet the needs of children (Bain, 1967).

The 1946 annual conference held in Cincinnati was significant for two reasons. It was the first annual conference held at a national level since 1942. More important, the organization again reflected its international focus in changing its name to the Association for Childhood Education International (ACEI).

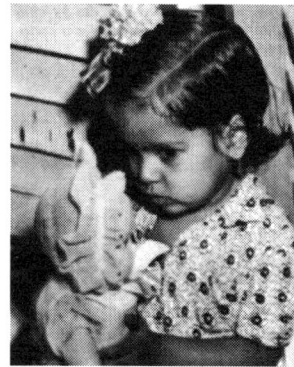

The international interests of the organization had persisted since its beginnings; moreover, service at the international level had been extended to war-torn countries after WW I. After WW II and under the leadership of Executive Secretary Mary E. Leeper, ACEI participants were challenged to perceive the organization's responsibilities at a worldwide level. Funds contributed by Patty Smith Hill were used to provide study grants in the United States for teachers from Europe. The first two recipients came from Norway in 1945, followed by two teachers from Germany in 1949.

More significantly, ACEI again participated in a project to serve children displaced by war. In cooperation with the United Nations Relief and Rehabilitation Administration(UNRRA), ACEI sponsored a project of sending toys to children displaced by war. UNRRA transported kits of toys collected by ACEI through appeals to branches. In 1946, a total of 489 toy kits were shipped to Austria, Yugoslavia, Greece and Italy. In addition, complimentary copies of *Childhood Education* and curriculum materials requested by Mildred English, Deputy Chief of the Educational Branch of the U.S. Office of Military Government, were sent to German curriculum and textbook centers (Bain, 1967).

Resolving Social Issues

As noted earlier, the efforts for equal educational and economic opportunity had limited success prior to the war's end in 1945. Despite efforts to desegregate schools and secure equitable pay for Black teachers, conditions remained unequal, especially in southern states.

Many members of ACE and later ACEI were Black or members of other minority ethnic groups, who encountered difficulties in full participation at organizational meetings in a country that practiced segregation. Black members' concerns about discriminatory practices at annual conferences first appeared in 1931 Executive Board minutes. In planning for the conference to be held in Washington, D.C., the Chairman of the Local Committee, Katherine Watkins, brought the issue to the attention of the board. The Executive Board minutes described the situation:

Miss Watkins presented the feeling of the Washington Negro members of our Association who were afraid that there might be some discrimination against them at meetings and social affairs since there is a race feeling in Washington. It came out in the discussion that the Executive Board acts for the National Organization and has no power to rule out nor formulate policies as the action of the social affairs of the locality in which the convention is held according to the constitution. The Washington colored members who have paid their dues as members are entitled to the same privileges as other members. Miss Abbot was empowered to write a letter to Miss Watkins setting forth our stand on the subject making clear that it is not the function of the Executive Board to decide as to the treatment of any sect, race or any other individual group. Its function as the Executive Board of a national organization is to carry out the provisions of the constitution. (Association for Childhood Education, minutes of Executive Board Meeting, December 1931, p. 6)

The Executive Board did not feel it could take action to put pressure on local agencies regarding discrimination; nevertheless, the following motion was passed: "The Executive Board request Miss Watkins to interview the manager of the Willard Hotel and ask him to see that all delegates receive courteous treatment" (Association for Childhood Education, minutes of Executive Board Meeting, December 1931, p. 6).

Another situation emerged in 1933 during planning by the Executive Board for the annual meeting in Nashville. Apparently the question concerned the advisability of holding a dinner at a Black institution. The minutes reflected the discussion as follows:

The dinner at the Negro Normal was now discussed. It was stated that it would not be embarrassing but would be an educational contribution from the convention. It was suggested that it would be a good thing to have the president of the Normal make a short talk on what had been done for the Negro in his school, etc. It was asked that the students give a program of music and stories. It was agreed that $1.00 or, if it was necessary so that the Normal could make something on the dinner, $1.25 should be

---

BITS FROM THE ACEI ARCHIVES: 1930-1950

Minutes of Executive Board Meeting
Monday, April 21, 1930

"Discussion of incidental expenses for Miss Hansen. Dr. Davis says she needs more space, as she works mostly in her bedroom. She has not used her monthly allowance for stenographic help etc. She has rented a typewriter at her own expense." (Miss Rowena Hansen had the position of Assistant to the Editor at a salary of $1500.)

Highlights of the Administration 1935-1938

"Marjorie Hardy's information received from Amy Hostler that anyone becoming a board member must immediately provide herself with a black lace dinner dress. The same Marjorie is letting down the hem to equip herself appropriately." (Reported by Helen Reynolds)

Minutes of Executive Board Meeting
April 4, 1942

A discussion of ways to help teachers in war responsibilities included the following:
"Miss Marble, Teachers College, Columbia University has a mimeographed booklet, "Fun in Air Raids.".

---

charged for the dinner. It was asked that they would not go to the trouble and expense of having souvenirs. At this time there was short discussion on the Negro and when they would be invited into the A.C.E. on the same footing. Miss Leeper stated that the Negro was already a part of the A.C.E. both as Branches and as individuals but that the treatment of the Negro at conventions depended on the town in which the convention was held and how all Negroes were treated in that town. This relationship in convention city would have to be made quite clear to them. (Association for Childhood Education, minutes of Executive Board meeting, December 1933, pp. 10-11)

In the postwar years, ACEI's position to establish equal conditions for all members was strengthened. Actions by the organization reflected a progressive attitude toward improvement of race relations. The issue of equal conditions for all members moved toward resolution in 1949 when the Executive Board was presented with two requests. The first, from three states with segregated schools, requested the organization recognize separate state associations for Black and White teachers. The second request, from a Black branch in Washington, D.C., asked the organization to require that conferences be held in cities where Black participants could receive equal treatment. The Executive Board's deliberations took place at the conference in Salt Lake City where accommodations for Blacks had been found to be very limited.

In regard to the request for separate state associations, the Executive Board met with representatives of the groups making the request, then acted to decide that only one association would be recognized from each state. A similar resolution was made regarding accommodations for Black members at annual conferences. Black representatives were invited to meet with the Executive Board to discuss problems and make suggestions for the 1950 conference in Asheville, North Carolina. Through the efforts of the Executive Board and local planning committee, many of the problems of accommodations and equal treatment of all members were corrected in Asheville.

Following the Asheville conference and a study made by the Committee on Conference Location, the request by the Washington Black group was resolved by a directive to groups who wanted to invite ACEI to meet in their city. The directive stated that the invitation should include a "statement giving assurance that Negro members and members from other countries can live in the same hotels as those used by other delegates and eat in all dining rooms without embarrassment" (Bain, 1967, p. 30).

The action by the Association reflected a new vision of the purposes and potential of the organization. This was but one example of the accomplishments that would be achieved by ACEI after 1950. In the next two decades, ACEI would experience its largest period of growth and continue its contributions to the field of early childhood education during a new era of interest in the potential of the early years for later development and learning.

CHAPTER 4
A GOLDEN AGE OF CHILDHOOD: 1950-1975

The nation that entered the decade of the 1950s was significantly different from the one that had existed in the early decades of the century. The demands of the Great Depression and World War II on the United States government resulted in an expanded role both in domestic and international affairs. Each year from 1950 to 1975, the federal budget was increased to fund the many programs and policies that responded to needs and problems of the day. These years were ones of progress in many areas of national and international affairs; but they were also years of turmoil, uncertainty, fear and violence as the United States and other nations struggled toward living within a global context that was to replace national boundaries.

INTERNATIONAL INVOLVEMENT

Although the end of World War II signaled an end to war on a global scale, hostilities did not cease. The United States and her allies were almost continuously involved in regional confrontations. The nation found itself increasingly influential in international affairs, partly through economic aid given to countries rebuilding from the devastation of war, but also because of the ideological polarity between East and West. The struggle between democracy and communism, or the cold war, permeated policies and practices in the federal government that influenced the direction of the United States for 40 years. The cold war grew out of a fear of communism and the concern that its influence would spread and control the world. Within that fear was a direct competitiveness between the Soviet Union and the United States as each country monitored the other to ascertain military, technological and economic dominance. The 1957 launching of Sputnik by the Soviet Union is now looked upon as a key event that affected the United States domestically and internationally in accelerating the effort to maintain leadership in the struggle for western dominance in the cold war. One response to the cold war was the maintenance of a strong military presence in both the United States and allied countries. American military forces continued to occupy Germany and Japan and were extended to other countries in the effort to protect the West from communism. The military budget grew as each side escalated the race to develop sophisticated armaments for use in event of war. By the 1960s, American military influence had spread to the point that more than 1.5 million military personnel were stationed in a hundred countries. The military budget exceeded $80 billion annually by 1972, with one worker in seven employed in defense projects (Henretta et al., 1987). This powerful military establishment had been organized into the Department of Defense in 1947, and led to a revolution in American government as the executive branch assumed authority over foreign affairs that paralleled the strength of military forces. In a centralized culture, the influence of the military and the federal government had an impact on the lives of ordinary people, both in the United States and in other countries where United States influence affected their domestic affairs. In his farewell speech (1961), President Eisenhower warned the nation that the military-industrial complex could endanger democratic processes if misused.

Some would propose that the United States misused its military power and influence during this period in the effort to contain communism. The Central Intelligence Agency, established in 1949, was involved secretly in the internal affairs of countries and successfully directed the overthrow of foreign governments in Iran and Guatemala. It was unsuccessful against Fidel Castro of Cuba in 1961 and Achmed Sukarno of Indonesia in 1958.

Although the policy of containment of communism met with mixed success, progress was made in the cold war. President John Kennedy successfully resolved the Cuban missile crisis in 1962 when Soviet missiles were removed from Cuba. In 1963, the United States and the Soviet Union agreed to a test-ban treaty. Instead of containment, President Kennedy proposed detente as a concept of foreign policy that accepted the Soviet Union as an adversary with whom the United States could negotiate. Coexistence of the two powers was the goal.

The fear of communism affected internal affairs in the United States. An anticommunist hysteria that became known as "McCarthyism" prevailed as Senator Joseph McCarthy of Wisconsin led a crusade against communist sympathizers. Investigation of suspected communists led to loss of employment for many, particularly in the entertainment industry. In a comprehensive investigation of federal employers in 1947, 6 million employees were subjected to security checks and 14 thousand were investigated by the FBI (Henretta et al., 1987). Antisubversion campaigns were conducted in state and local governments, universities and businesses. Senator McCarthy became the most vocal anticommunist. His excess in investigating suspected communists finally led to his censure by the Senate.

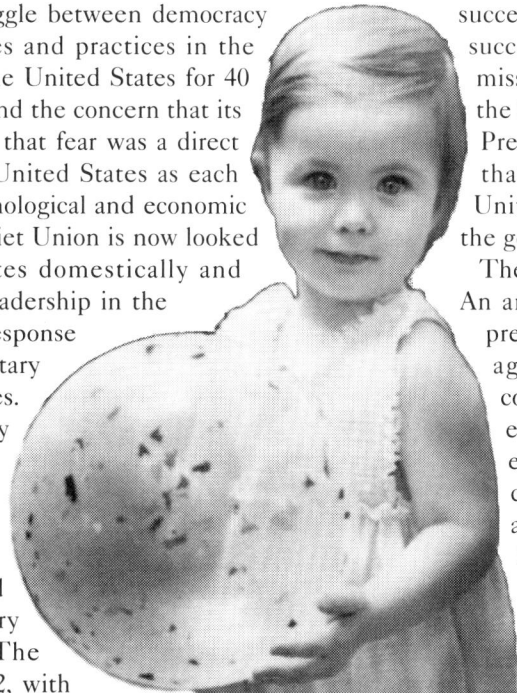

DOMESTIC ACHIEVEMENT

Indirectly, the fear of communism also had positive effects for segments of the population between 1950 and 1975. The launching of Sputnik accelerated interest in space exploration, followed by substantial funding that allowed the United States to compete in the race for space. The competitive nature of the space race generalized into concerns for better research and education in the United States. Money for universities and schools was increased as the government supported technological and scientific innovations, along with improved schooling that would ultimately enhance accomplishments by graduates of institutions of higher education in the United States.

Raised sensitivity to civil rights, plus activism among minorities and women, resulted in social, economic and educational changes that had positive effects for children and families from all segments of the population. Nevertheless, much of the legislation and programs of the period targeted the needs of minorities and the poor. President Eisenhower followed Truman's efforts to integrate the schools. With President Kennedy's call for a "New Frontier," space exploration was funded and a spirit of patriotism was sparked through the Peace Corps, which saw young American college graduates serving to improve the life of citizens in underdeveloped countries. In addition, the Department of Health, Education and Welfare was established.

If Kennedy's "New Frontier" established the momentum for social change, Lyndon B. Johnson's "Great Society" held the record for the most major legislative accomplishments impacting on the life and education of Americans, particularly minorities and the poor. After Kennedy's assassination in 1963, Johnson used his influence in Congress to pass comprehensive legislation intended to improve various aspects of American life. Among his legislative accomplishments were the Civil Rights Act of 1964, Voting Rights Act of 1965, Elementary and Secondary Education Act, and establishment of health care for the elderly and poor through Medicare and Medicaid. Federal urban renewal and home mortgage assistance facilitated improved housing and home ownership; expansion of the National Park System widened the availability and protection of national areas of beauty and natural significance. The Highway Beautification Act encouraged the protection of highways from commercial exploitation; and establishment of the National Endowment for the Arts and National Endowment for the Humanities encouraged the fine arts, literature and drama through financial support at the federal level.

Social growth did not occur without pain and turmoil. The civil rights

CHILDHOOD IN THE UNITED STATES:
Not only do today's children live in quite a different world from that in which their parents and teachers grew up; they also face an unprecedented future, since the rate of social change and its impact on learning and living cannot be left out of account. Furthermore, there are cumulative implications in the recent findings of inquiries into human behavior, human development, human aspirations and human relations. They constitute further challenges to continuing forward adjustment in provisions for child nurture and education. These considerations, coupled with the tensions and pressures which characterize this age of unremitting scientific advance and world-wide industrialization, make adaptability to change quite as essential to survival and fulfillment as backgrounds of knowledge and competence.–Laura Zirbes. (1959). What should we know about learning? *Childhood Education*, 36, 153.

movement, which brought the right to vote and equal opportunity for employment and education, was accomplished at a cost of harassment, imprisonment and murder as White backlash sought to maintain the status quo. John Kennedy's assassination was followed by the killing of two civil rights leaders, Martin Luther King, Jr. and Medgar Evars, as well as many civil rights workers. Robert Kennedy was also shot and killed as he campaigned for the presidency in 1968.

Civil rights activists, themselves, became violent. Abandoning the peaceful activism espoused by early civil rights leaders, Black activism became more militant, particularly in urban areas. Fueled by the Black Muslim movement and other militant groups, Black riots in northern cities between 1964 and 1968 undermined White support for the civil rights movement.

By the end of Lyndon Johnson's administration, the motivation for social legislation and civil rights had ebbed. The accumulated cost in U. S. lives and dollars and allied involvement in the Vietnam War resulted in the loss of support of the American people. What had begun as funding and military advisers for South Vietnam under Kennedy became full-scale troop and armament commitment under Johnson. A counterculture of youth protesting the war was joined in opposition by mainstream citizens and politicians. Domestic dissent over the war caused Johnson to decide against seeking another term as president. The defeat of American troops in Vietnam, plus the protracted efforts to extricate the United States from the war, caused a national psychological wound that persisted through the next decades. The enormous expense of the war and a large federal deficit eventually caused Americans to pull out of the war, in defeat, in January 1973 during Richard Nixon's presidency. Although Johnson probably is best remembered for his leadership in a misguided war, he should also be remembered for his efforts for the poor that came to be called the "War on Poverty."

CHILDHOOD IN THE UNITED STATES: 1950-1975

The title of this chapter refers to childhood as being in a golden era. When compared to previous historical periods and the years to come toward the end of the century, it was, perhaps for a brief period, a time of many advantages for children. It was an optimistic period economically. At the beginning of the 1950s, the majority of women with children under the age of 6 worked in the home if economic circumstances permitted. The United States was in a consumer-oriented period as families acquired homes, cars, appliances and goods that were again abundantly available. Time payment arrangements made products accessible to segments of the population who could not have accumulated the cash to acquire items such as refrigerators or television sets. As a result of the GI Bill, veterans had an opportunity for a college education that, in turn, translated into a higher percentage of the population entering a middle-class lifestyle.

Family lifestyles were changing for many Americans. The acquisition of cars, televisions and radios brought events and trends closer to home. Television viewing afforded a common experience to all socioeconomic groups. Improvement of the highway system encouraged family travel, also paving the way for construction of motels, hotels and entertainment centers such as Disneyland. Suburban areas continued to expand because home ownership was more affordable.

In the 1970s, family camping became popular as a recreation option. Community recreation programs developed with opportunities available for both adults and children. The national interest in sports extended to organized sports for children, particularly young boys, as Little League baseball teams were organized in both urban and rural areas. Local businesses sponsored ball teams accessible to boys and girls of all income levels.

By the advent of the 1970s, social changes were evolving that would change forcefully family structures, lifestyles and economics. Childhood would become a different experience as the divorce rate rose steadily and mothers entered the workplace in increasing numbers each year. The economic hardships of living in a single-parent family structure and the adjustment to having mothers employed in both intact and divorced families revolutionized family lifestyles and children's childhood experiences. Day care became a necessity that would result in its expansion into a major industry in the 1980s.

There were growing concerns about the negative effects of television on children. The quality of programming was questioned, and initial research on the effects of lengthy viewing and inappropriate programming for children began to cause concern for child specialists.

Another side of childhood began to emerge with information on rising rates of child abuse and the phenomenon of babies born to drug-addicted mothers. By 1975, the American lifestyle and childhood had moved into a different direction in history as the solution of some negative conditions affecting children were replaced with new concerns.

Conditions of Childhood

After the end of World War II, the birthrate escalated rapidly in what came to be known as the Baby Boom. By 1970, the birthrate had dropped significantly as working mothers reduced the size of their families and young professional women postponed childbearing in favor of career advancement. Baby boomers affected the nation at every step of their growth as schools, manufacturers and other facets of the American society and economy sought to provide services and goods for this large segment of the population. Conditions for these children and those who came after them in the 1960s and 1970s were substantially improved through advances in health services that developed during the same decades.

Improvements in Child Health. Significant progress was made in control of communicable diseases. Availability of penicillin, sulfa drugs and antibiotics made it possible to treat tuberculosis, mastoiditis, meningitis, osteomyelitis, pneumonia and other bacterial infections. Development of the Salk and Sabin vaccines almost eliminated poliomyelitis as a cause of death and physical handicap (Public Health Service, 1976).

There was concern during the period that not enough doctors, pediatricians and other health services were available for baby boomers. Advances made in treating infants and children were not widely available because of shortages in medical workers. An example was surgery for congenital heart defects in infants. To widen the availability of this new medical procedure, regional centers and state crippled children programs were established to provide open heart surgery for congenital heart defects.

Numerous national voluntary organizations focused their efforts on the health needs of children. The National Society for Crippled Children and Adults served individuals who lacked normal functioning of the neuromuscular and skeletal system; the United Epilepsy Association and National Epilepsy League served about 275,000 children and youth under 21 years of age. The Allergy Foundation of America estimated that 14 percent of all children had allergic diseases. The American Hearing Society reported that 1.3 million school-age children were hearing impaired. The National Society for the Prevention of Blindness, American Optometric Association's Committee on Visual Problems of Children and Youth, United Cerebral Palsy Association and Muscular Dystrophy Association were additional foundations that included children in the health services they provided (Public Health Service, 1976).

The needs of mentally retarded children were also addressed when parents organized the National Association for Retarded Children, later to become the National Association for Retarded Citizens. In 1957, Congress appropriated $1 million to the Children's Bureau for grants to states to develop diagnosis and treatment methods for retarded children. President Kennedy, who had a mentally retarded sister, heightened national visibility on the needs of the mentally retarded. The Maternal and Child Health and Mental Retardation Planning Amendments of 1963 included comprehensive maternity and child health care service, as well as multidisciplinary training of specialists to work with the handicapped and retarded.

The concern about poor or nonexistent prenatal care, particularly among the urban poor, led to establishment of maternal and infant projects to serve expectant mothers early in pregnancy and continuing through the first months of the baby's life. About 57,260 women were served during the first year. Maternal and infant programs were joined by similar ones when grants were made available in 1965 that would provide comprehensive health services for preschool and school-age children. Dental health projects provided preventive dental care, and intensive care projects initiated life-supporting systems for at-risk newborn babies.

In 1961, President Kennedy established a Center for Research in Child Health in the Public Health Service, which was renamed the National Institute of Child Health and Human Development in 1962. Among its accomplishments was development of a method to screen newborns for inborn metabolic errors that could lead to mental retardation. The screening for phenylketonuria (PKU) quickly become required through state legislation.

By the 1970s, improved health services had accomplished much to protect the health of the nation's children. The infant mortality rate had been lowered and the gap in health care for minority and poor children had been narrowed, but not eliminated. Tuberculosis had been reduced in Native American and Alaskan populations. On the negative side, socioeconomic problems of the 1970s gave rise to new health concerns. The use and abuse of drugs, increased venereal disease, adolescent child abuse, lead poisoning and the growing number of severe accidents resulting in injury and death posed new challenges in health care. In addition, hunger and malnutrition were still prevalent among children of the poor (Public Health Service, 1976).

Institutionalized Children. In 1950, abuse and neglect in child-caring institutions were being reported, a situation that still existed in isolated settings in the 1970s. Although efforts had been made for many decades to reduce the number of children in institutionalized care, about 28,000 remained in 1970. Beginning in 1972, an effort was made to further deinstitutionalize as many children as possible. Efforts were made to return children to community settings in the belief that their potential for reintegration into the community is better served in small group homes or foster care. Between 1965 and 1975, the Department of Health, Education and Welfare offered grants leading to deinstitutionalizing dependent children, as well as mentally retarded, emotionally disturbed and disabled children. Institutions for children in need of specialized treatment replaced general institutions. The most difficult-to-care-for children continued to be served in the specialized institutions (Datta, 1976).

Foster Care and Adoption. Although numbers of children in foster care decreased in the 1940s, the 1950s again saw larger numbers of children whose parents were unable to care for them. These children, however, needed care as the result of social pathology in the home rather than economic need in the family. Children needing foster care in the 1970s meant specialized training for foster parents and support of social workers. Placement of older, more difficult children indicated a trend for longer term foster care that constantly strained the system.

Costs of foster care increased, and the lack of appropriate foster care placements made it difficult to provide long-term quality care for children who spent the majority of their childhood years in out-of-home placements.

While numbers of children in foster care increased between 1950 and 1970, the number of children available for adoption decreased. Many parents turned to obtaining babies illegally or through directly negotiating with the expectant mother. These alternatives resulted in high financial costs and increased legal risks for the adoptive parents. There was also a greater uncertainty about the physical and mental characteristics of the adopted child.

Children with special needs were still available for adoption but difficult to place. To find homes for these children, agencies became more flexible and creative in their adoption policies. Trans-racial and single-parent adoptions were permitted. Age restrictions were relaxed and subsidized adoptions were initiated. In 1975, over 40 states had approved subsidized adoptions where adoptive families could be given a grant to help meet the expenses of raising the adoptive child. In 1971, 169,000 children were adopted, 50 percent by relatives. The median age for adoption was 2 months and only 12 percent of children adopted by a non-relative were other than White (Datta, 1976).

Child Welfare. The 1935 Social Security Act (Title IV), which included Aid to Families with Dependent Children (AFDC), was amended in 1967 to provide benefits through training and job placement services for heads of households eligible for AFDC. The broadened services of these child welfare services included the prevention of neglect, abuse, exploitation and delinquency of children, as well as strengthening the home environment and/or providing for children's care in foster care or day care facilities. Between 1960 and 1972, the number of AFDC increased from 3.5 million to over 11 million.

Much controversy surrounded AFDC. One concern in 1975 was over the escalating costs of the program. Another was whether working poor below the poverty level should receive benefits and whether employment of adult recipients should be required. Criticisms of the program included concerns that benefits varied from state to state and that some recipients received benefits for an extended number of years. In states with high benefits, employment was not advantageous; benefits were almost as high as the income of the working poor.

The effectiveness of welfare policies was questioned by many at that time. What had originally been intended as a source to stabilize families and provide for the welfare of poor children had instead become a source of dependency for AFDC recipients. The consensus seemed to be that the child welfare system needed to be changed; but there was little agreement on how to correct the problems, achieve some control over escalating costs and still ensure a minimum level of support for needy children (Datta, 1976).

Child Abuse. The existence of widespread child abuse first received attention in 1946 when a published report suggested that accidental injuries to infants and children could have been inflicted by parents. The concept of the "battered child"

(Kempe, 1962) brought widespread attention to the problem. In 1974, the American Humane Association Survey estimated that over a million American children suffered physical abuse or neglect and possibly 20,000 children a year died from mistreatment (Fleming,1976). In January 1974, the Child Abuse Prevention and Treatment Act authorized a National Center on Child Abuse and Neglect that was charged to compile information on abuse, conduct research on the causes of abuse and operate a clearinghouse on promising programs in the identification and prevention of abuse. Passage of the act demonstrated recognition that child abuse was a national problem. While most child welfare services focused on the needs of children of the poor, child abuse affected children in all socioeconomic categories; moreover, it was a national problem that would resist solution in the years after its official recognition in 1974 (Datta, 1976).

Children of the Poor:
Focusing on Problems of Minorities and Poverty

As had been true throughout history, not all children lived comfortable, middle-class lives during this "golden age of childhood." Growing up as a child in a minority group or at the poverty level or both meant a different type of childhood experience. Two minority populations in particular, Mexican nationals and Puerto Ricans, increased the numbers through immigration during the period. Although efforts were made in 1950 to curb illegal entry by Mexican nationals, seasonal workers were admitted as migrant workers through Bracero programs. Between 1948 and 1964, 4.5 million Mexican nationals entered the United States. Puerto Ricans, who as American citizens could freely enter the United Sates, were also employed as migrant workers on the east coast. Beginning in 1950, the Puerto Rican population began to grow rapidly (Snapper, 1976).

Children of minorities and the poor benefitted during the 1950s because of the efforts of civil rights activists and the federal government. For a period of two decades, national attention was focused on the disparate needs of these children in an effort to eradicate poverty and inequity and improve education. Although poverty still persisted in the 1970s, when funding for federal efforts for the poor was substantially reduced, the effectiveness of intervention programs established under the War on Poverty has been supported by longitudinal research.

The War on Poverty was part of President Johnson's efforts to build the Great Society. Legislation passed during his tenure affected families and children from all economic backgrounds; nevertheless, Johnson expressed a commitment to end the disadvantages experienced by poor children.

Poor people made up about a fourth of the American population; three-fourths of the poor were white. The poor in the United States were isolated farmers and miners in Appalachia, country folk recently uprooted from the land, blacks mired in urban ghettos, Hispanics in migrant labor camps and urban barrios, native Americans on reservations, women trying against all odds to raise families on their own, and the abandoned and destitute elderly. (Henretta et al., 1987, p. 881)

The War on Poverty was initiated with passage of the Economic Opportunity Act of 1964. This omnibus bill funded Head Start, a preschool program to prepare disadvantaged children for public school, and the Job Corps and Neighborhood Youth Corps to train youth. Another program, Upward Bound, had as its purpose to prepare low-income students for college. Social Security benefits were raised and extended to include more occupations; Aid to Dependent Families and the Food Stamp program provided assistance to low-income families. While programs funded under the Economic Opportunity Act and other legislation of the period did not end poverty, the lives of thousands of children were influenced and their potential for a more productive life improved as a result of the War on Poverty.

Minority Children and the Civil Rights Movement

The civil rights movement benefitted minority and poor children. Although Blacks had worked through activism to improve their working conditions during World War II, the civil rights movement acquired momentum after the 1954 Brown vs. Board of Education of Topeka decision ruled racial segregation in the public schools unconstitutional. The ruling triggered resistance to school integration, but it also encouraged Blacks to renew their efforts for civil rights through nonviolent protest. The Civil Rights Act, outlawing discrimination in public accommodations or employment based on race, religion, national origin or sex, was passed in 1964. The Voting Rights Act of 1965 banned literacy tests that had been used to prevent Blacks from registering to vote. Legislation improving civil rights did not immediately end the resistance and violence, but the positive effects of the laws were felt by minority children and their families over a period of time.

Moreover, the civil rights movement spread to other minority groups. Hispanics organized the Mexican American Political Association and the more militant Brown Berets. A political party, La Raza Unida, was initiated to promote Hispanic interests. Similarly, Cesar Chavez organized the United Farm Workers Union to represent migrant laborers. Native Americans organized through the American Indian Movement that engaged in militant confrontations to draw attention to Native American issues. Lawsuits to reclaim Indian lands illegally taken in violation of federal laws and treaties resulted in economic gains and public awareness of injustices. Although the more militant actions of minority activist groups may have been counterproductive in initiating equity for minority populations, the legislation passed in response to awareness raised by the movement made a permanent difference in equal access to voting and public facilities and improvements in education and employment (Henretta et al., 1987).

CHILDHOOD EDUCATION: GROWTH AND CHANGE

The period from 1950 to 1975 was characterized by growth and change at all levels of education. Innovation and expansion of curriculum were supported by an unprecedented level of federal and state funding. As a result, schooling in the United States had the resources to accept the challenges of new expectations for educating students of all ages.

Growth and Change in Higher Education

Two sources of funding made university education available to larger numbers of students. The G.I. Bill of Rights provided scholarships to WW II veterans who might not have had the opportunity to attend college otherwise. The National Defense Act of 1958, Higher Education Act of 1965 and Higher Education Amendments provided loans and grants to low- and middle-income students, again enabling many new populations of students to acquire degrees in higher education.

The increase in numbers of college students meant that the population of students in colleges and universities would be more diversified. The number of women students increased by more than 50 percent during this time. Enrollment of minority students also increased; however, enrollment of Black students and other minorities tended to be limited in many universities until civil rights legislation forced institutions of higher education to open their doors to minority applicants. Likewise, there was limited representation of women and minorities on college and university faculties during the 1950s and 1960s (Cremin, 1988). Availability of federal money for research fueled growth and change in higher education. Large amounts of money were granted universities, expanding the types of research conducted during these decades of ample funding. Departments in natural sciences and medicine were able to obtain both government and foundation grants that allowed them to become powerful within their institutions.

Universities also broadened the programs available to students. Newly professionalized occupations, such as police administration and hotel management, were incorporated into university curricula. The shift toward a more practical education for a wider population of students became a trend. Courses in archery and tennis were added to the college curriculum and remedial courses offered to

MILGRIM HIGH

What is Milgrim High like? It is a big, expensive building, on spacious but barren grounds. Every door is at the end of a corridor; there is no reception area, no public space in which one can transition from the outside world. Between class periods the corridors are tumultuously crowded; during them they are empty; but they are always guarded with teachers and students on patrol duty. Patrol duty does not consist primarily in the policing of congested throngs of moving students, though it includes this, or the guarding of property from damage. Its principal function is the checking of corridor passes. Between classes, no student may walk down the corridor without a form, signed by a teacher, telling where he is coming from, where he is going, and the time to the minute, at which the pass is valid. A student caught in the corridor without such a pass is taken to the office where a detention slip is made out against him, and he is required to remain at school for two or three hours after the close of the school day. He may do his homework during this time, but he may not leave his seat or talk.—Edgar Z. Friedenberg. (1988). The high school. In T. J. Crimmins & N. L. Shumsky (Eds.), *American life, American people.* San Diego: Harcourt Brace Jovanovich, pp. 181-182.

TOWARD EQUALITY IN AMERICA

In America we can build a house, built by caring adults, big enough to share with and nurture all our children. It is up to each of us to contribute to that house in the way we feel most confident—some can help lay the foundation, others can nail in planks, add bricks, put in pipes, build the roof, depending on your skills and resources. The important thing is to care and to act effectively where you are with what you have.—Marian Wright Edelman. Expanding Roots. From an address to the ACEI Annual Study Conference, Charlotte, NC, 1977.

students whose potential to pass university work was questionable (Cremin, 1988).

Beyond the colleges and universities, an extensive range of alternative education sources became available. Private institutions offered vocational training for various occupations ranging from business skills to electronic and vehicle repair. Museums, libraries, historical societies and zoos were but some of the institutions that offered more informal educational opportunities. Printed materials extended the range of possibilities for information through books, magazines, journals and newspapers (Gross & Gross, 1976).

Growth and Change in Secondary and Elementary Education

Public schools continued the process of consolidation after World War II. Urban schools became increasingly centralized with a single superintendent exercising power over curriculum and instruction, personnel and administration. As smaller districts consolidated under legal mandate, the number of school districts decreased at the same time that the size of the consolidated school districts increased. Compared to 117,000 local school districts in 1940, there were 41,000 districts in 1960.

By 1975, the success of public schooling was supported by statistical evidence. The number of years of schooling increased as did the number of days children spent in school. In 1940, the American adult, 25 years of age or older, had completed 8.6 years of schooling; the years completed rose to 12.5 by 1980. Likewise, public school averaged 144 days in 1900, but had increased to 178 days by 1980 (Cremin, 1988).

Advances were made in teachers' salaries and education. In 1960, 62 percent of teachers held bachelor's degrees, while 24 percent held advanced graduate degrees. Twelve years later, the percentage with bachelor's degrees remained the same, but the percentage holding graduate degrees had risen to 38 percent. Teachers' salaries rose from an average of $5,174 per year in 1960 to $13,895 in 1976. Teachers' organizations were larger and more effective. The two largest, the National Education Association and the American Federation of Teachers, worked effectively with boards of education for improved salaries and benefits for teachers (Cremin, 1988).

Public school organizational patterns in curriculum and instruction changed in the two decades following WW II. Prior to 1950, the junior high school had been separated from the elementary school. General dissatisfaction with this organizational pattern continued for several decades, with dialogue centering on the role and curriculum of the junior high school. In the 1950s, the concept of the middle school became more popular because it served students in late childhood and early adolescence together (Richardson, 1985).

Expansion and transformation of curriculum included the conversion of history, geography and civics into the social studies. Reading, writing, speaking and literature became the language arts; and biology, physics, geology and chemistry became general science. More instructional attention was given to the arts, physical education and vocational education, while drivers education was added to secondary school curriculum.

Toward Equal Opportunity in Education: Education of Minorities, the Poor and the Handicapped

The civil rights movement, combined with advances in educational pedagogy, focused attention on the educational needs of various high-risk populations, including minorities, the handicapped and children who were experiencing low levels of achievement in school. Through civil rights legislation and federal funding for compensatory programs, extensive efforts were made to better serve the educational needs of high-risk student populations.

Effects of Brown vs. Board of Education. The inequities in housing and schooling for minorities, particularly Blacks, were well known after World War II. A report, based on the 1940 Census, described the inequalities in educational opportunities and educational achievement between Caucasians and Blacks in the District of Columbia and the 17 southern states. Blacks were receiving less in every aspect of educational services: length of the school year, pupil-teacher ratios, teacher salaries, school accommodations, equipment, special services and advanced education (Cremin, 1988). Separate but equal education had never been a reality.

The Brown decisions of 1954 and 1955 placed the government on the side of desegregation. Although the Supreme Court decisions were fought for many years, 91.3 percent of all southern Black students attended biracial schools by 1972. In the border states, 76.4 percent attended biracial schools; and in the North and West, 89.1 percent. The Civil Rights Act of 1964 facilitated desegregation, providing the Attorney General authority to undertake legal action to protect the rights of Blacks through school desegregation and barring discrimination in public accommodations and employment (Cremin, 1988).

James Farmer (1976) described the impact of the Brown decision on the civil rights movement:

The Brown decision set in motion boundless energies, spawned by the promise of Jeffersonian equalitarianism but pent up by delay in fulfilling that promise. From Little Rock to Alabama to Oxford, Mississippi, and throughout the South, children and youth rose of irrepressible and heroic dimensions and the barriers came down. There were of course other foci in the equality drive of the 1950s and 1960s. There were boycotts and Freedom Rides and sit-ins at lunch counters; voter registration drives were launched and, with Federal support, blacks were registered en masse; Dr. King, whose charismatic appeal succeeded in activating a sizable minority, perhaps one-fourth, of the black population, as well as millions of whites, led marches for across-the-board desegregation and dignity, and there was the March on Washington in 1963–all stimulated by the decision that educational facilities by race were unconstitutional. (Farmer, 1976, p. 196)

Compensatory Education. Equity in education for other minority groups came through Lau vs. Nichols in 1974. The court ruling directed school districts to establish special language programs for non-English-speaking children. Congress passed the Bilingual Education Act in 1974, providing funds for bilingual education for children falling within the Lau ruling.

All disadvantaged children were affected by the Elementary and Secondary Education Act of 1965, part of the Great Society legislation under Lyndon Johnson. Seen as antipoverty measures that would promote educational equity for poor children, the act provided federal funding to assist schools in their education. The programs funded by this legislation and the Bilingual Education Act in 1974 were part of a large body of programs designed to provide compensatory education. Funding was also provided for migrant children and schools affected by desegregation. All were designed to assist low-income, minority and low-achieving students improve their chances for success in school learning.

Education of the Handicapped. In the early decades of the 1900s, residential schools were developed to educate children with special learning needs. As more was learned about these children, the residential schools were found to be costly and frequently guilty of abuse and neglect of the students. Raised expectations for handicapped children, plus the growing conviction that these special children also had an equal right to education, led to state and federal funding to provide a first-class education for the handicapped.

In the 1960s and 1970s, separation and isolation of handicapped children were seen as similar to segregation of minority children. The growing conviction that children with special needs would do better if they were educated alongside their age-mates in the public schools led to passage of the Education of All Handicapped Children Act of 1975 (P.L. 94-142). The most dramatic provision of the act mandated that handicapped students be mainstreamed as much as possible with their normal peers. The law asserted that handicapped children had a right to an education in the least restrictive environment that would meet their individual needs. Schools were required to screen, diagnose and plan for the individual needs of each student (Morrison, 1988). In the years between 1975 and 1990, public schools worked through the difficulties in transitioning from programs for handicapped children in self-contained classrooms to mainstreaming these children into regular classrooms (Cremin, 1988).

Effects of Federal Programs on Public Schools. Legislation to fund schools for programs for compensatory, bilingual and desegregated education resulted in the development of innovative programs for poor, minority and handicapped children. Programs developed for children with special learning needs were influenced by trends in educational thinking and educational psychology that evolved between 1950 and 1975. Elementary school curriculum and instruction were also affected by the Head Start models and, later, Planned Variation Follow Through programs funded to provide elementary school programs for students who had participated in Head Start. These programs included individualized instruction, team teaching, open education concepts and parent involvement components —some of the innovations introduced in the research-based models of the 1960s and 1970s. Many promising instructional methods were first developed in the field of early childhood education and adapted for the elementary school. The years between 1950 and 1975 were marked by an abundance of ideas, resources, programs, models and opportunities for teachers to incorporate new curriculum practices into their classrooms. It was a period of optimism and enthusiasm for improving the learning for all students, and a time of challenge to understand the requirements and benefits of multiple, federally funded programs that existed side-by-side in elementary schools, especially those schools serving high percentages of low-income and minority students.

EARLY CHILDHOOD EDUCATION:
INNOVATIONS FOR INTERVENTION AND COMPENSATION

I spent the entire morning of my first day at kindergarten seated on a wooden horse. Unlike the merry-go-round stallions or the mechanical saddle horse at the A&P, it was homely, stationary and constructed from a barrel. Although it was not a very comfortable seat, it enabled me to see the entire classroom without feeling any pressure to participate. At recess time, my teacher waited until the other children filed out before inviting me to come outside and see the playground. I climbed down. On that day and in

THIS DAY'S CHILD IN SCHOOL

Who is today's child? Is there a composite creature who shares a common growth pattern, a common cultural experience, and a common set of values that allow us to talk about the child today in a special way? I suspect that there is and there is not.

No more than a generation ago it was possible for teachers to say with a sense of comfort and control that middle-class children did not have, and were not expected to have, difficulties at school that could be attributed to a group phenomenon such as wholesale unreadiness because of cultural difference. If Alicia was not able to listen and learn, it was because she had not worked out the confusion over her adoption; if Chris had trouble reading, it was because of the conflict between his loyalty to his semi-literate housekeeper and his educated working mother. But middle-class children were expected to learn, and learn they did for the most part. The exceptions only proved the rule . . .

Who is this day's child? Is it the middle-class children who, although still holding their own to a great extent, are developing a syndrome new for them—learning disability and/or learning disaffection? Or is it the poverty children, who have not responded en masse to the enticements to do well at school, although a higher percentage of them are entering college than ever before? In communities all over the nation, middle-class children and poverty children are both getting remediation, and both are dropping out of school. Tuning out of learning in the school style is appearing as early as first grade in different kinds of communities.—Dorothy Cohen (1974). This day's child in school. *Childhood Education, 51,* 8.

the weeks that followed, I recognized that Miss Klingensmith was competent, caring, and insightful. When I played school, which was often, I always insisted on being Miss Klingensmith. That early experience touches my life deeply even now.—Mary Renck Jalongo. (1988). Mentors, master teachers and teacher induction. In G. L. Roberson & M. A. Johnson (Eds.), *Leaders in education* (p.90). Lanham, MD: University Press of America.

Unlike the original kindergartens established for poor immigrant children in the 19th century, the kindergartens of the 1950s were characterized as most suitable for the middle-class child. New theories of development and learning that emerged in the 1950s, combined with the new attention to early education of poor and minority children, launched early childhood education into an era of renewal and transformation that Evelyn Weber (1969) characterized as resulting from "pressures for change."

The Challenges of the Great Society
for Early Childhood Education

The federally funded intervention programs of the 1960s had as their goal to improve school achievement for poor and minority children. These programs were grounded in the concepts of *intervention* and *compensatory* education. Intervention was based on the philosophy that poor children would benefit from early experiences prior to entry into public school. The concept of early intervention could be traced, historically, to Maria Montessori's work in slum neighborhoods in Italy; the McMillan sisters' work in England with their nursery schools for poor English children; and kindergartens established in urban slums in the United States through settlement houses, churches and philanthropic sources (Spodek, 1973). In the 1960s, intervention implied efforts to alter the poverty cycle that tended to persist from generation to generation.

Funding for programs under the category of compensatory education was based on the concept that poor and minority children needed specialized instruction above and beyond the regular public school curriculum. Bilingual education along with mainstreaming of handicapped students provided supplemental instruction beyond that normally provided in public schools. In early childhood, education intervention and compensatory education were efforts to break the poverty cycle through specialized programs provided at the preschool level. While Head Start programs are the best known early childhood intervention projects, there were many others that included infant-intervention programs and parent education programs (Gordon, Guinagh & Jester, 1967).

With the advent of Head Start and other early childhood intervention programs, the challenges of the Great Society included infants and preschool children and their families. Funding for these programs coincided with the availability of new theories on development and learning that had been emerging in the 1950s. The work of a new generation of child development specialists and psychologists was used as the foundation for the development of many models developed for Head Start programs (Day & Parker, 1977).

Toward New Theories of Learning in Early Childhood Education

Renewed interest in the potential of the early childhood years for enhancing development and learning emerged concurrently with new and continuing sources of information about development and learning in the 1950s and 1960s. Some theorists such as B. F. Skinner and Erik Erikson were extending the earlier work of Thorndike and Freud. Others took new directions as research revealed more information about how young children develop cognitively. Jean Piaget's studies on cognitive development influenced a new generation of psychologists and educators who translated theory into practice in early childhood education.

In the 1920s, Thorndike's learning theory influenced the kindergarten reform movement. B. F. Skinner supplanted Thorndike's work in behaviorist psychology in the 1950s and 1960s. Skinner was concerned with the shaping of behavior through operant conditioning, which used reinforcement strategies to increase the rate of occurrence of desired responses. Undesirable behaviors, likewise, could be extinguished through the absence of reinforcement. Skinner believed that reinforcement is the most influential determinant of behavior, that all human behavior is externally caused and controlled. Behavior modification, therefore, was advocated for teachers and parents to shape the child's behavior. In instruction, subject matter is organized in a logical sequence and broken into manageable steps. Each step is reinforced in the learner by strategies to assure desired learning. Programmed instruction with appropriate conditioning was the learning model Skinner recommended for instruction of students of all ages (Skinner, 1953).

MANUEL AND MICHAIL

During a free play period Manuel, knowing English words for only three colors, selected a bright purple disk from the counting set and asked the teacher's aide the English term for the color. Manuel took the disk to a friend sitting at the same table and spoke the color "name" in English. He then put the disk in his pocket, while looking for a puzzle. Later he took the disk to the teacher, told her the color in English, put the disk in his left hand and got a drink of water. After the drink Manuel went to the boys in the block corner where, speaking in Spanish except for the word "purple" he showed them the disk. He placed the purple disk in the small dump truck and left it there. Later in the day when the teacher was preparing for an art class by asking each child to select a sheet of construction paper by color in English, Manuel asked for "a purple."

During a math class, as the children were taking turns counting different sets of supplies in the room (paint brushes; jars of paint and paste; boxes of paper, puzzles, crayons, chalk, clay and games), Michail's turn came. He counted the eleven rubber farm animals "one" to "six" in English and "siete" to "once" in Spanish.—Betty L. Broman. (1972). The Spanish-speaking five-year-old. *Childhood Education, 48,* 362.

While Skinner's learning theory extended the work of Pavlov, Watson and Thorndike, Erikson extended Freud's work in personality development. He focused on stages of personality development throughout the life cycle. Within the first three stages, the infant and young child must develop a sense of trust, autonomy and initiative. As the child matures through the stages, favorable or unfavorable results occur, depending on whether or not the child was successful in resolving the crisis of each stage. Positive resolution of each stage of personality development results in desirable qualities; conversely, negative resolution of a stage can have long-lasting personality effects later in life.

Erikson's psychosocial theory emphasized the individual's adaptation to social demands. The child who developed a healthy personality was able to develop a balance between his own desires and the demands of the environment. In *Childhood and Society* (1950), Erikson discussed the relationship between the individual ego and society. He was concerned with the psychological hazards the child lived with in contemporary society and the sociocultural relationships in the family and community that affected the child.

Cognitive psychologists in the 1950s developed new concepts of the relationship between environment and intelligence. The work of Piaget marked a shift in understanding about the importance of the child's experiences in the environment in influencing cognitive development. This concept that intelligence responded to experience influenced American psychologists, particularly Benjamin Bloom and J. McVicker Hunt who focused on the significance of the early years for cognitive development in their own research.

Jean Piaget began his study of cognitive development in the 1920s, but it was not until his writings were translated into English that his theories became well-known. In the 1960s, his influence caught on with great rapidity at the same time that American society was looking to education to improve the intellectual effectiveness of the poor. The tenet perceived by American scholars, that the nature of the experiences provided a child could make a difference in the child's intellectual development, gave hope to a growing expectation that education could resolve the problems of families living in poverty. Moreover, and because Piaget recognized the infant as an active initiator of learning rather than a passive learner, there were those who proposed that educational intervention should begin in children's earliest years.

Piaget's theory of stage-changes in an individual's way of knowing is sometimes described as a cognitive-interactionist theory. He determined that knowledge is constructed and reconstructed as the individual acts upon the environment. The learner's responses to new information are dependent upon the stage of cognitive development.

The child moves through four stages of cognitive development: sensorimotor, preoperational, concrete operational and formal operational, each one characterized by qualitative differences in the child's thinking. Knowledge is constructed through assimilation, accommodation and equilibration. Assimilation is the process of encountering and taking in new information into an existing scheme. Through accommodation, the scheme (knowledge structure) is modified by the inclusion of the new experience. Equilibration is the balance between assimilation and accommodation. According to Piaget, assimilation and accommodation lead not only to reorganization of knowledge, but also to different ways of thinking. His theory suggests that motivation to learn comes from within the individual (Piaget, 1963).

Piaget's cognitive-developmental theory differed significantly from Gesell's maturational and Skinner's behaviorist theories of learning. It emphasized the role of the child as an active participant in the learning process and opened new ways of understanding how to enable that process in educational programs for children.

Benjamin Bloom's contributions to educational thought centered on the influence of the environment in learning. In *Stability and Change in Human Characteristics* (1964), he reported longitudinal research to support his thesis that the early years are a significant period of intellectual development. He proposed that variations in the environment are particularly influential during the first five years, and suggested that these differences were related to cognitive growth during that time. Deprivation during the preschool years, therefore, could have serious consequences for both cognitive and affective development. Bloom believed that appropriate preschool experiences could affect significantly the young child's patterns of learning.

J. McVicker Hunt further explicated Piaget's theory of cognitive development in *Intelligence and Experience* (1961), when he questioned the assumption that intelligence is fixed. He also expressed doubts about traditional approaches to the education of young children that avoided excessive stimulation. He proposed that early experiences were important for the development of intelligence and that a substantially higher adult level of intellectual capacity could be achieved by providing quality encounters with the environment in the early years. In other

A GOOD BEGINNING HAS NO END
The preschooler's best preparation for school is to be provided with all the opportunities he needs to live and learn as a preschooler, to experience widely and intensely what is relevant and appropriate to that stage. The current pressure by parents to start academic work in nursery school and kindergarten means robbing the child of his childhood, depriving him of learning by direct experience and by spontaneous activity which he needs if he is to cope effectively with requirements of academic programs later.–Lawrence K. Frank. (1959). A good beginning has no end. *Childhood Education,36,* 3.

words, intelligence is modifiable.

Dr. Maria Montessori, the first female physician in Italy, began her work with children as director of a state-supported school for "defective" children in Rome. She was influenced in her work by Jean Itard and Eduoard Seguin who worked with deaf and mentally deficient children. Montessori developed instructional materials that were manipulative and sensory for use with mentally retarded children. When she expanded her work to educate children of the poor through Children's Houses in tenements in Rome, she brought her didactic materials to these schools.

Montessori stressed the importance of structure in the learning environment. The learning environments in her classrooms were highly organized with carefully sequenced, self-correcting materials that emphasized the interaction between sensorimotor activity and cognitive development and facilitated the child's independence (McCarthy & Houston, 1980). She also emphasized respect for the child whose life must be recognized as separate and different from adult life; therefore, education should be individualized to match the child's unique nature. She characterized children as having absorbent minds (Montessori, 1967) that use sensory impressions from the environment to develop the senses. She supported the notion of sensitive periods when children can learn specific skills more easily, as well as advocated that children should be able to educate themselves within the environment through auto-education (Morrison, 1988).

The Montessori method was first introduced in the United States before World War I. The movement expanded during the 1920s but declined during the depression years, becoming popular again in the 1950s. Two organizations, the Association Montessori Internationale (AMI) and the American Montessori Society (AMS), each with differing philosophies of the Montessori method, developed Montessori programs in the United States (Spodek, Saracho & Davis, 1991).

Early childhood educators in the 1960s were bombarded with an avalanche of research, programs, funding opportunities, informational resources and materials available for use with young children. Opposing theories of learning were touted as the optimum route to improve the learning potential of young children. Personality and affective development joined cognitive and physical development as factors to be considered in developing preschool programs. The importance of play assumed prominence with its role in personality development and learning. Expression and creativity in preschool programs needed to be considered, as well as the unique learning needs of children of the poor, who Martin Deutsch (1963) proposed were not culturally prepared to attend middle-class schools. Research and implementation of early childhood education, funded through intervention and compensatory programs within the War on Poverty, afforded opportunities for theorists and early childhood specialists to develop many new models of education for poor, minority and handicapped children. These would affect the education of all young children for the rest of the 20th century.

Federal Role in Early Childhood Education

The federal role in early childhood education was initiated in the 1960s through passage of the Economic Opportunity Act, which created the Office of Economic Opportunity. Project Head Start, administered through the Office of Economic Opportunity, began as an eight-week summer program in 1965 (Butler, 1965). Approximately 550,000 children were served in 2,500 centers. The design for the program came from a panel of child development experts gathered by the federal government in 1964 to provide a program that encouraged learning patterns, emotions, skills and attitudes that would protect children against the pattern of poverty (McCarthy & Houston, 1980; Morrison, 1988; Spodek, Saracho and & Davis, 1991).

Head Start soon became a year-long program. It was joined by a Migrant Program, Home Start and Project Follow Through. Project Head Start continues to be a comprehensive program that includes appropriate learning experiences, health care, meals and parent education. Medical and dental examinations, immunizations and dental work are provided for children. A social services coordinator helps parents locate community agencies when assistance is needed; and parents are encouraged to become involved in the program by serving on policy-setting committees, in workshops and as volunteers with classroom activities. The Home Start program extended parental training and participation in early education into the home (McCarthy & Houston, 1980).

Project Follow Through was developed to help schools receiving Head Start children make the transition into the primary school. Funded in 1967, the program served children from low-income families enrolled in kindergarten through 3rd grade. A similar program, Project Developmental Continuity, also sought to promote greater continuity between Head Start programs and the public schools Head Start children would attend. This program was funded in 1974 by the Administration for Children, Youth, and Families (ACYF), but was discontinued in 1981 (Morrison, 1988).

Planned Variation Head Start and Follow Through Models

Head Start and Follow Through funding led to a search for programs that would enhance the intellectual and academic performance of poor children. The new programs developed for the Planned Variations research project required innovative educational approaches to early education. Model programs reflected the competing theoretical positions of the educators who designed them. In 1968 and 1969, the Office of Education sent out program descriptions of the models to Head Start directors and districts wishing to commit to Follow Through programs in their schools. The models presented varied curriculum, materials and instructional techniques to foster learning goals of disadvantaged students. Although the models presented sometimes bewildering options for early childhood programs, the period was remarkable in terms of educational possibilities. Model sponsors were able to use both existing and emerging theoretical positions in determining the philosophy and goals of their model. Funding was available to pilot and implement the models at various sites around the United States. Later some of the models were packaged with curriculum materials and made available to both public and private early childhood programs (Weber, 1984).

Never before or since in the history of early childhood education was an era of innovation and change so quickly accomplished or so well funded. Never before had a variety of philosophies and approaches to early childhood education been developed simultaneously and disseminated so widely. Descriptions of only a few of the models exemplify their diverse nature of model development.

Two Head Start models grounded in behaviorist learning theory were Bushnell's Behavior Analysis model and the direct instruction model of Bereiter and Engelmann and, later, Becker. The goals and objectives of each program were specified in terms of observable behavior. Rewards were given to children contingent upon the production of "correct" behaviors. Bereiter, Engelmann and Becker used intensive direct instruction with a strong emphasis on verbal responses (Bereiter & Engelmann, 1973). Curriculum materials designed specifically for the program were used for instruction in reading and mathematics.

The Intensive Learning Model at the University of Georgia and the Demonstration and Research Center for Early Education (DARCEE) were additional models based on behaviorist learning theory (Weber, 1984).

Child-centered models focused on the importance of the child's involvement in planning and implementing instruction. Some of the programs were based on Piaget's theory of cognitive development that focused on the child in active roles. The High/Scope Cognitively Oriented Curriculum, Lavatelli Program and Kamii-DeVries Curriculum were models that were grounded in Piagetian theory.

The High/Scope program used a curriculum framework based on what was described as key experiences. Teachers planned an environment and curriculum that would encourage children to be actively involved in these learning experiences. Curriculum matched children's cognitive stage and provided activities that incorporated concepts from concrete to abstract and simple to complex. The sequences helped organize the curriculum for children to experience learning in action and in representational activities so as to construct new concepts (Hohmann, Banet & Weikart, 1979).

The Lavatelli Program focused on children's important cognitive development of classification, space, number and seriation concepts. Lavatelli designed a detailed program and materials in her Piagetian curriculum that included a teacher's manual and manipulative materials for the lessons. The goal of each lesson was for the children to engage in thinking and problem-solving (Morrison, 1988).

Kamii's Piaget-Derived Preschool Curriculum was not a set curriculum; rather, the aim of the program was to help the child move toward intellectual and moral autonomy. Objectives of the program included physical knowledge, logico-mathematical knowledge, structuring of space and time, social knowledge and representation. The teacher's role was to structure situations that would encourage children to seek knowledge, use curiosity, solve problems and act independently (Kamii, 1973).

There were other Head Start and Follow Through models that were child-centered, but were not derived from a single theory of learning. The Responsive Model Program (Nimnicht, 1973) used the learning environment as the curriculum for the child. The materials in the environment were autotelic or self-rewarding. The objective of the program was to help children learn how to learn. The teacher's role was to set up the environment and facilitate children's use of materials to learn.

The Tucson Early Education Model, designed for Hispanic children in the Southwest, had language competence, intellectual base, motivational base and societal arts and skills as major objectives. Individualized instruction, small group activities, learning centers and interrelated skills instruction were teaching strategies used in this program.

There were models that reflected a variety of influences. Montessori models reflected that philosophy, while Open Classroom programs were adapted from British Infant School practices based on the work of Piaget and Dewey. The Bank Street Model focused on language development and thinking as one of its purposes and used sensory experiences and picture storybooks to serve as catalysts for learning and conversation between teachers and children (Biber, 1973).

Project Follow Through was initiated in 1967 to expand Head Start practices into kindergarten and the primary grades. Follow Through used specialists to

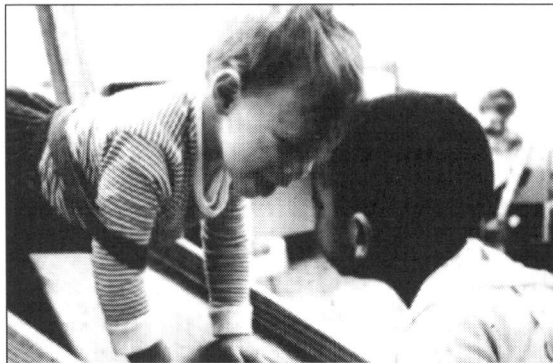

LIFETIME LEARNINGS HAVE FRUITFUL BEGINNINGS
First-grade teachers say they can always spot the children who have been to nursery school or kindergarten. . . But no one can promise-without-fail that any one specific gain will show up always in every child. Children don't "learn" to cooperate in kindergarten. This can't be taught in kindergarten–this is a lifetime learning. All that fours and fives can do is to make a fruitful beginning. Children don't learn self-confidence in kindergarten–this is a life's task, not a grade's task. But they do make a beginning. They make a beginning–a four- and five-year-old beginning–in science, in arithmetic, in social studies, in health, in art, in music, in industrial art, in philosophy, in psychology. . . yes, in reading and writing too! But pre-primary education can only do its job, whatever its fours and fives are ready for. It cannot guarantee that every child will be ready to read next year when he is six. Or be disciplined next year when he is six.–James L. Hymes, Jr. (1962). The importance of pre-primary education. *Childhood Education, 39*, 8.

develop innovative models in the primary grades. Follow Through models addressed the needs of at-risk students who had been through Head Start and were in danger of losing the gains they had made prior to entering elementary school. Follow Through programs hoped to maintain the benefits of Head Start.

Models developed for infants and toddlers took several forms. One approach focused on infant and toddler day care. Centers were established at universities to determine the efficacy of providing quality care for very young children. Examples are the demonstration center at the University of North Carolina (Keister, 1970), the work of Willis and Ricciuti (1975) at Cornell University and the Children's Center at Syracuse University (Honig & Lally, 1981).

Other infant and toddler programs sought to prevent later learning problems through intervention. Some of the programs served only children, while others worked with parents or the parents and the child. Some programs provided instruction in the home, while others were center-based. Examples of these models are the Karnes Home Intervention Program, Family Development Research Program, Levenstein's Mother-Child Program and Schaefer's Infant Education Program (Day & Parker, 1977). The parent education approach used by Ira Gordon at the University of Florida was unique in that parent educators were used to teach other parents in the home and later in home learning centers. Extensive use was made of neighborhood settings and peers as instructors (Gordon, 1977; Gordon & Breivogel, 1976).

In 1975, funding for model development efforts was diminishing. Early research reports on the success of Head Start were discouraging, as gains in learning seemed to be lost in the elementary grades; however, longitudinal studies would later show positive long-term effects for both Head Start and other programs for disadvantaged children (Consortium for Longitudinal Studies, 1983). After 25 years, children who had participated in Head Start were found to do better in school, were less likely to repeat a grade or be placed in special education classes. They were less likely to drop out of secondary school and more likely to attend college. And in spite of the decline in funding for compensatory and intervention research and programming after 1975, Head Start continued to serve children, even though the numbers of children needing the program far exceeded the capacity of Head Start programs to provide desirable preschool experiences.

Day Care: Custodial or Educational?

Day care has had a mixed history of private and public support. Philanthropic nursery schools performed a custodial care service for poor children. In contrast, nursery schools established at colleges and universities and at tuition-financed schools as part of the child study movement provided models of early education for young children. Federally funded day care programs were developed as a response to a societal need. When that need was resolved, the funding for such programs was eliminated (Morrison, 1988; Ranck, 1990).

In the 1950s, the prevailing perception was that the need for child care was an individual family problem, that child care service programs were for the poor or for families who were inadequate. Women who had entered the workforce during depression and war years would now return to the home because men could resume responsibility for supporting the family. In reality, this was a false impression. By 1966, 24.2 percent of married women with children under the age of 6 were employed. The need for day care would continue to increase and private sources would fill that need for middle-class families (Cremin, 1988).

The philosophy of child care was uncertain during this period. The tradition of protective care, developed by philanthropic nurseries and depression era WPA schools, was in conflict with the nursery school programs based on child development research. Day care for protection versus day care for development of children needed to be resolved. The Day Care and Child Development Council of America, established in the 1960s, made efforts to combine the two concepts. Nine volumes on day care programs were introduced by the Office of Child Development to assist in the goal of improving day care programs (Grotberg, 1976). In spite of these efforts, the major source for advances in child care came as the result of the Head Start movement.

The emerging trend of more women entering employment, combined with advances in child development and knowledge asserting the importance of the preschool years for future learning, resulted in new interest in a cognitive development focus in day care programs. The intervention and compensatory efforts of the War on Poverty, as implemented in Head Start programs in the 1960s, demonstrated the importance of educational programs in the early years and provided potential solutions to the custodial versus child development philosophies that were in conflict for day care programs (Grubb & Lazerson, 1988).

Federal funding through welfare reform in the 1960s did provide day care

CHILDHOOD EDUCATION CENTER DEDICATION DAY, AUGUST 14, 1960
The building dedication is the result of many people working together for a definite purpose. The human interest stories of this endeavor are varied and often thrilling. There were those individuals who: volunteered a monthly gift "for the duration"; baked bread for friends; gave stock certificates; sent deeds for property later sold for several thousand dollars; donated earnings from baby-sitting; sent book royalties; gave money saved by an abbreviated vacation; donated dividends; gave income from guest riders in autos; shared honorariums. Others gave hours and days and weeks and years of volunteer labor. To do this some members traveled far and lived in Washington at their own expense. These gifts and many others were offered in the spirit of the sacrificial first gift of five thousand dollars presented fifteen years ago by the late Isabel Lazarus, then a retired Baltimore teacher. When presenting it she remarked, "Maybe some day this will help ACEI have its own library."—Mary Esther Leeper, Moving Forward. From a talk given on Childhood Education Center Dedication Day, August 14, 1960.

services for a population of poverty children. The Department of Health, Education and Welfare administered legislation in the 1960s to bring welfare mothers into the labor market. The Manpower Development and Training Act and AFDC funding required employment training for eligibility to receive welfare. Child care was provided within these two programs. Later, consolidated under Title XX of the Social Security Act, publicly subsidized child care programs expanded to more than 200 in the 1970s. Nevertheless, day care provided under these programs focused on employment for parents rather than quality programming for the children being served (Prescott, 1974).

In 1975, the issue of custodial care versus early childhood programming from a child development perspective still had not been resolved. Federal Interagency Day Care Standards, based on information gained from Head Start child development concepts, had been introduced in 1968. Acceptance of the standards, however, continued to be controversial as day care programs questioned the value and expense of implementing such programming for the population of children they served (Grotberg, 1976; Grubb & Lazerson, 1988).

ACEI, A PERIOD OF GROWTH AND EXPANSION: 1950-1975

In a sense, the organization's fortunes paralleled the positive period for children and childhood education between 1950 and 1975. ACEI experienced its largest membership during this period, as well as expansion of publications made available to the field. The organization's strength was reflected in the purchase of property and construction of a headquarters building. On ACEI's 75th anniversary in 1967, the membership was able to look with pride upon the accomplishments and growth of the organization since its beginning in 1892.

After 1967, the Association's fortunes took another turn when ACEI experienced a loss of membership and revenues that affected its ability to continue services at the same level as before. By 1975, the sharp decrease in members forced the organization to restructure and reconsider how best to serve its mission in a changing world for children and childhood education.

Construction of ACEI Childhood Education Center

Much of the energy and work of the Association between 1950 and 1960 revolved around establishing a national headquarters and planning activities and services that would be possible once the ACEI Center became a reality. In 1952, at the Annual Study Conference in Philadelphia, the first steps in accomplishing the dream were taken when the Board proposed such a building. Members not only approved the venture but raised more than $1,000 toward expenses. In 1955, a Steering Committee on Permanent ACEI Headquarters was appointed at the Annual Study Conference to engage in planning for the project. By August, the Steering Committee had outlined the functions that a space should provide beyond the concept of a headquarters. It would be a Childhood Education Center, rather than an office building, one that would serve both as a laboratory for adults who work with children and as an expanded headquarters office.

The search for property took three years. Because of the many restrictions in the Washington, D.C., area, the Steering Committee encountered numerous disappointments in finding the right piece of property. In the meantime, voluntary contributions toward the purchase of property and construction of a facility continued. Finally, in 1957, land was purchased; property that met the organization's requirements had been located on Wisconsin Avenue and Quebec Street. Plans for the center were approved by neighborhood residents and zoning authorization granted by the District of Columbia. When it became known that construction must begin within the year after zoning authorization, an accelerated building plan schedule to secure the $400,000 needed was presented at the 1958 Annual Study Conference in Atlantic City. In response to the call for additional funds, members pledged both large and small amounts of money, enabling the Association to float a construction loan and secure a contractor (Bain, 1967).

In February 1960, ACEI moved to the new center. On August 14, 1960, on a Sunday afternoon, the center was dedicated, followed by a two-day conference of ACEI State/Province Presidents, Advisory Committee Members and Branch Representatives. Only six years later, at the 1966 Annual Study Conference in Chicago, full payment of the loan was marked with a symbolic burning of the mortgage.

Service Through ACEI Childhood Education Center

One of the attractive features of the ACEI Center location was its proximity to children. There were two public schools nearby, as well as the National Child Research Center and various other private schools, nursery schools and preschools. In response to requests from members and branches, the first floor of the center housed a changing display of art, science, toys, equipment, books, maps, globes and other materials. An expanded program featured demonstrations, workshops and meetings that attracted visitors from many countries around the world. Exhibits from other countries were included in the roster of informative programs available from time to time. The post of Mary E. Leeper Fellow to coordinate center activities was established in honor of Mary Leeper, Executive Secretary from 1930 to 1952. As a result of the expanded program, children visited the center frequently to participate in demonstrations, try out commercial equipment, and enjoy the exhibits and programs prepared for both children and adults.

With the larger space available within the new building, the Association was also able to expand its work in more traditional areas. Publications could be produced and stored more effectively, making it possible to consider a wider range of titles to be published each year. Membership records and services could be accommodated, as well as better office space and furnishings for staff members. The historical records and memorabilia of the organization were organized and shelved for accessibility by members and researchers. At last the Association had the space needed to activate the many types of service it had in mind at local, national and international levels.

ACEI and the New Federal Programs

One thing we owe all children is a situation where they can think their own parents are beautiful, without having to denigrate the way other children's parents look. The corrective for "white is beautiful" is not "black is beautiful." The corrective is "white is beautiful; black is beautiful; red, yellow—and some sects add green—are beautiful." My people in New Guinea added the green. When they talked about the people of the world, they would say all together, "Black, white, red, yellow and green." When asked if they had ever seen anybody who was green, they said, "Not yet!" I hope you have seen the cartoon where little green men from a flying saucer were looking at our latest space effort flying out to outer space. The caption: "They'll never believe this at home."– Margaret Mead. Uniqueness and Universality. From an address to the ACEI Annual Study Conference, April 1974, Washington, D.C.

As in previous historical periods, the Association was actively involved in programs enacted by legislation at the national level. Through representation at important meetings and events, participation in advisory committees and cooperation with other organizations, ACEI was represented in key decisions forthcoming from the federal government with regard to childhood education in the 1960s.

Passage of the Economic Opportunity Act in 1964 meant expanded involvement of the Association. Center staff participated in the planning stages of the Head Start program and contributed in the early implementation stages. ACEI publications relevant to training of Head Start personnel were made available. Complimentary kits of ACEI publications, appropriate for training Head Start staff, were sent to all Project Head Start Training Centers. The ACEI Center also opened a Resource Room to provide demonstrations and exhibits of appropriate materials and experiences for preschool children that were useful for Project Head Start programs.

The Association maintained an interest in Project Head Start policy and practice. The progress of the program was a concern, and leaders communicated with policymakers when they felt decisions being made were detrimental to children enrolled in Head Start. In June 1966, ACEI joined with seven other national organizations in issuing a statement expressing concerns for the administration of federal programs affecting young children. The statement further recommended "that the staffs of federal agencies responsible for initiating and funding programs for young children include professionally trained specialists who would cooperate in developing criteria for funding, approval of proposals and continuous evaluation of operating programs" (Bain,1967, p. 70).

An Expanding Role for Publications

ACEI's active role during this period of influence was reflected in the quantity and quality of its publications. In addition to *Childhood Education* and various other books and booklets that appeared from year to year, leaflets intended to influence educational practices were added to the publications list. The flyer *What Are Kindergartens For?*, originally published by the New Jersey State Department of Education, had 190,000 copies distributed by 1966. Two other popular titles were the portfolio *Creating with Materials for Work and Play* and the bulletin *Equipment and Supplies* that has been updated and reprinted in recent years. An increasing number of bulletins, portfolios and other practical materials were in wide demand by teachers and other practitioners in the field.

Childhood Education also included articles that were relevant to the trends and issues of the times. Two issues were dedicated to national leaders: the January 1953 issue to Eleanor Roosevelt and the January 1964 issue to President John Kennedy. The international influence of *Childhood Education* was reflected in its distribution in over 75 countries. The Educational Press Association of America awarded the journal the 1963-64 Eleanor Fishburn Award for its outstanding contribution to international understanding.

Significant books were published by the organization during this period. *Feelings and Learning*, replete with photo essays as well as text, was in such demand that it was reprinted less than a year after the original printing in 1965. *Readings from Childhood Education: Articles of Lasting Value* contained reprinted articles from 1924 to 1964 to commemorate the 40th year of the journal's publication. The *Umbrella Books* series continued to be in demand. Many more significant ACEI publications were used by teachers and other adults working with children both in preschool and elementary school settings.

After the 75th Anniversary: 1967-1975

When ACEI celebrated its 75-year history in 1967, it was a time to reflect upon seven decades of successful service and ongoing concerns for children. The Childhood Education Center was paid for and being used for a multitude of useful and significant purposes. Membership exceeded 80,000. ACEI was an organization of national and international influence that seemed destined for continuing success in its future. Yet, shortly after 1967, membership began to decline, a decline that became a hemorrhage by 1975. The reality of that loss in members and influence cannot be overlooked because it, too, is part of the organization's history. Various factors contributed to the problem, but it might be simplistic to try to point to one policy, event or trend that determined the fate of the Association for the next 25 years.

One reality was that ACEI for many years was the only national organization available for elementary teachers. This changed with the establishment of organizations for specialized areas of the elementary school curriculum. Associations for elementary mathematics, language arts, science and social studies

offered services for teachers who were interested in information and networking in those content areas. Undoubtedly, many professionals found it necessary to make a decision between membership in one organization or the other, rather than belonging to several associations.

The growth of early childhood education programs in settings other than the public schools also was a possible factor. The organization had had a large membership comprised of public school teachers, college and university faculty who prepared teachers for public schools. With the advent of federally funded preschool programs and the steady increase in day care facilities, the field of early childhood education broadened and became more specialized. The National Association for the Education of Young Children became an important organization for preschool programs, especially child care, in the 1960s and 1970s.

A 1966 constitutional revision also affected ACEI membership. Prior to that time, classes of membership included international, life and branch. Branch membership was considerably less expensive and did not require subscription to *Childhood Education*. The constitutional revision eliminated these membership classes, established a single membership that included a subscription to *Childhood Education* and increased the dues accordingly. Faced with the more expensive membership cost, many branch members failed to understand and appreciate the need for a consistent membership fee, including the journal subscription with its significant value.

Other factors may have contributed to the downturn in the fortunes of ACEI; the archives do not reveal clues as to what those might be. Indeed, some of the explanations stated above are the result of interviews with longtime members of the organization and not any clear, substantiated evidence. Regardless of the cause or causes, the following 25 years of the Association, as it has sought to find its new niche in a changing field of childhood education, have been full of challenges. A more streamlined organization has emerged with a solid core of members who are committed to the purposes of the organization and have a firm belief in its role in the future of children and childhood education.

CHAPTER 5
A CHANGING WORLD
CHILDHOOD AND EDUCATION RECONSIDERED: 1975-1992

As Americans moved toward the middle of the decade of the 1970s, morale was low. The Vietnamese War that had raised public opposition under Lyndon Johnson continued under his successor, Richard Nixon, who was also unable to effect a positive resolution of the war. Public opposition to the war escalated after 1970, particularly among college students who led demonstrations on many campuses. The invasion of Cambodia triggered campus rioting at Kent State University that resulted in the deaths of four students (Garraty, 1983).

There was a division among the American people. Those who supported the war (Hawks) were opposed by those who felt Americans did not belong in Vietnam (Doves). The conflict was exacerbated by the negative stance taken by the Executive branch of the government against dissidents and demonstrators. The signing of the 1973 Peace Accords did little to heal the country as Americans observed the continued defeat of South Vietnam.

Despite growing concerns about the failure to make progress in winning the war, Nixon was reelected in 1972. The conduct of the President and some of his staff during that period, however, further divided and demoralized the nation as the result of events that came to be known as "Watergate." Revelations about various illegal activities led to the resignation of Nixon aides, staff members and, finally, Nixon himself in August 1974. Vice-President Agnew had already been forced to resign the previous October and Gerald Ford had succeeded him.

The Vietnam War finally ended under Nixon's successor, President Ford, following the fall of Saigon in April 1975. Ford inherited a country rocked by scandal and defeat, as well as inflation partially caused by an Arab oil embargo against the United States after a brief war between Israel and the Arab states. The oil shortage not only drove up the price of gasoline, but inflation as well (Henretta et al., 1987). It would be many years before notable improvement could be made economically and politically in a nation that was sorely troubled.

INTERNATIONAL CONCERNS

Not all international interactions were unsuccessful. In February 1972, President Nixon had traveled to the People's Republic of China to lay the groundwork for reinstating a diplomatic relationship with that Communist government. The same year he made a trip to Moscow to sign a strategic arms limitation treaty (SALT I). President Carter, who took office after defeating Ford in 1976, was able to continue some diplomatic successes. Among his accomplishments was a treaty with Panama that would gradually transfer the Panama Canal to that nation. He also ended official recognition of Taiwan that further restored relations with Communist China. In 1979, ambassadors were exchanged with the People's Republic of China and another strategic arms limitation treaty (SALT II) was signed with the Soviet Union (Garraty, 1983).

President Carter's careful moderation of talks between Anwar Sadat, President of Egypt, and Prime Minister Begin of Israel resulted in a successful negotiation of a peace treaty in September 1978. Through the treaty that became known as the Camp David Agreement, Israel promised to withdraw from territory captured from Egypt during the "six-day war" in 1967. Egypt became the first Arab country to recognize Israel as a nation.

Carter experienced a significant failure in diplomacy, however, when the Ayatollah Khomeini seized power in Iran and drove the Shah into exile. When Carter allowed the Shah into the United States for medical treatment, Muslim students took 53 American hostages at the U. S. embassy in Teheran. The hostages were held 444 days and finally released on January 20, 1981, the day Ronald Reagan succeeded Carter as President.

The hostage crisis marked an unprecedented low in American influence in international affairs that was not appreciably improved when President Reagan supported conservative efforts in Nicaragua and El Salvador and invaded the small island of Grenada to overthrow the Cuban-backed regime. His decision to send a contingent of U.S. Marines to Lebanon, to keep the peace following Israel's invasion of Lebanon, also had a negative effect when 241 Americans were killed in a car bomb explosion in their Marine barracks in 1983. In 1990 and 1991, international affairs took a more successful turn after the Communist regime crumbled in Eastern Europe. The Cold War ended with the removal of the Berlin Wall, the reunification of East and West Germany and the overthrow of

Communist governments in countries within the Soviet Union. At the time of this writing, the fate of countries in Eastern Europe was still to be determined. It is uncertain how much credit could be given to American influence for the failure of Communism in Eastern Europe. Certainly, American pressure failed to protect students in the People's Republic of China who were demonstrating for a democratic government in 1990.

The freeing of Kuwait in early 1991, after invasion and occupation by troops serving under Saddam Hussein of Iraq, can be attributed to significant American influence and action. The brief Gulf War between Iraq and combined forces under the auspices of the United Nations had the benefit of leadership from the United States; however, the long-term outcome of the conflict named "Desert Storm" also was uncertain in the latter months of 1991.

DOMESTIC CONCERNS

When Carter took office in 1975, the nation was in the midst of a recession and other economic problems that prevailed throughout his administration. Inflation, accompanied by rising prices, soon had a serious effect on the poor and people on fixed incomes. Interest rates also rose. When Congress raised the minimum wage and adjusted Social Security payments to the cost of living index, the intent was to give relief to populations affected by inflation; conversely, there was a further upward pressure on prices. As people's wages and salaries went up in response to inflation, their income put them in higher tax brackets. The federal budget began to show larger deficits as the government spent more each year in response to inflation. The Federal Reserve Board adopted a tight-money policy that caused interest rates to go even higher. The high interest rates were particularly damaging to the automobile and housing industries when higher monthly payments depressed sales. Furthermore, the slump in the housing industry resulted in unemployment for thousands of construction workers (Henretta et al., 1987).

President Reagan hoped to replace high inflation with price stability. Using a philosophy of "supply-side economics," he checked the growth of federal spending and cut taxes in an effort to encourage investment and saving. Although recession and an unbalanced budget were the immediate result, there was some improvement in interest rates, inflation and unemployment by 1983.

While there were cuts in many areas of domestic spending, the defense budget was increased through a five-year commitment of $1.7 trillion that further increased the federal debt. Reagan also moved to lessen the impact of government regulations by deregulating some federal agencies that were established in the 1970s. Although some stability was restored to the nation's economy, it was at the expense of the poor. Tax reforms favored the wealthy; cuts in social programs reduced services needed by the poor. In 1982, more than a sixth of all Americans lived below the poverty line, a 13 percent rise over 1980. In 1984, the budget deficit rose $200 billion annually. Even though the Gramm-Rudman Balanced Budget and Emergency Deficit Reduction Control Act of 1985 required a balanced budget by 1991 (Henretta et al., 1987), there was little hope that it would be achieved. A recession, signaled by savings and loan and bank failures in states dependent on the oil industry, was followed by a broader recession in 1990 and 1991 that affected the nation as a whole. Widespread banking failures especially taxed the government's ability to absorb banking losses through federal insurance.

Advances in technology had a positive impact on economic expansion. The electronic computer had the most significant influence on both business and personal uses. Computers simplified and speeded progress in almost every area of work because of the ease of storing and retrieving information. On a larger scale, automation of industry was made possible when factory production and management of sales could be controlled by computer. Increased use and design improvements brought the purchase price of computers within a reasonable range for smaller businesses. Computers for personal use became an established segment of the computer industry market as programs for family budgets, income tax, word processing and educational software made it a logical tool for home and school use.

In the late 1980s, there was a growing concern about the loss of technological research and marketing to other countries, particularly Japan. Japanese manufacturers were gaining steadily in sales of automobiles and electronic goods in the United States. Beginning during the gasoline shortage, as a result of the Arab oil embargo, and continuing through the 1980s, increasing numbers of economical cars produced by Japanese, German and Korean manufacturers were purchased by American consumers. Electronic merchandise made by Japanese corporations, such as television sets, video recorders and video cameras, began to dominate sales in the United States. By 1991, Japan, Germany and other countries were investing in more research and design of new products than American companies. There was a serious concern that the United States would lose technological leadership to other nations.

The decade of the 1980s also was marked by a growing concern for the environment. Rising consumption of petroleum for transportation and manufacturing released smoke and other polluting gases into the atmosphere. Insecticides, toxic wastes and various types of packaging materials were affecting the environment by poisoning the earth and inundating it with increasing tons of trash each year. The difficulty of safe disposal of radioactive wastes and nuclear accidents, such as the one in the Soviet Union at Chernobyl, led to a decline in interest in the development of nuclear power sources (Garraty, 1983). By the advent of the 1990s, consciousness of the need to conserve resources and protect the environment was global; nevertheless, action to correct environmental concerns was small compared to the size of the problem. Only massive changes in manufacturing, lifestyle and population growth were likely to effectively manage and protect the environment and its resources.

CHILDHOOD IN THE UNITED STATES: 1975-1992

Children growing up between 1975 and 1990 experienced a different kind of childhood than the generation that preceded them in the 1950s and 1960s. Children of the 1970s and 1980s grew up during a period when family structure and lifestyles were changing. Whereas there had been a period of national focus on children and their education during the 1950s and 1960s, other priorities competed with that interest after 1975 (Keniston, 1975). The composition of the family changed, as well as the family lifestyle. Demographic changes helped to explain how childhood was experienced differently in a changing society. The trend was summarized as follows: "A statistical portrait of the United States in the 1970s and 1980s shows that Americans are living longer, having fewer children, divorcing more often, congregating in metropolitan areas and enjoying better access to education" (Henretta et al., 1987, p. 973).

Demographic Changes

By 1980, 75 percent of Americans lived in urban areas. Major growth in the continental United States was in the West, Southwest and South, with a corresponding decline in population in the East and Midwest.

The size and composition of families were affected by the declining birthrate and the rise in divorce rates. In 1920, the average household had 4.34 persons; by 1980, the average was only 2.75 people. The Baby Boom of the 1950s and 1960s was followed by two decades of declining birthrates until, in 1975, the birthrate was at the lowest point in the history of the United States. By 1980, birthrates rose with some of the increase attributed to working women over 30 who had delayed having children (Henretta et al., 1987; Hymes, 1991).

The rise in divorces was dramatic during the same period. In 1977, almost half of all marriages ended in divorce. Marital instability was one of the factors that led to a rise in single-parent households and the increase in

CHANGE IN THE CITY
What is truly remarkable is that the social intercourse which used to be the city's main function has now entirely vanished. The city is either crowded with the traffic of people and cars in a hurry or it is totally empty. Around noontime, office workers in business districts sometimes take an old-fashioned stroll when the weather is nice, and enjoy a piece of cake or an ice cream cone in the sun. But after five o'clock the streets are deserted. Nor do the streets in residential neighborhoods become correspondingly crowded, except around shopping centers and their parking lots. People return to their homes, as turtles withdraw into their shells. At home they enjoy the warmth of family life and, on occasion, the company of carefully chosen friends. The urban conglomerate has become a mass of small islands–houses, offices, and shopping centers–all separated from one another by a great void. The interstitial space has vanished.–Phillippe Aries. (1988). The family and the city. In T. J. Crimmins & N. L. Shumsky (Eds.), American life, American people, Vol. II (p. 177). San Diego: Harcourt Brace Jovanovich.

THE MALL
Walter Johnson High School in Bethesda, Maryland, was once in the middle of what was, literally, a cow pasture. There were cow pastures all around it; the team mascot was "Mighty Moo." But when Marcia was in ninth grade, that suddenly changed. And so did everything else.

Because up the hill from the school the Montgomery Mall appeared. A big two-level shopping mall, with four major department stores and the full lineup of other shops–the usual suburban bread-and-butter mall built in its time, about 10 years ago. Nothing outrageous or spectacular. . . but suddenly the students at Walter Johnson could not remember what they did on Saturday afternoon besides call each other up around 1:00 p.m. to ask, "Going to the mall?"

The girls would go shopping at Garfinckel's and Hecht's and the ladies' specialty and shoe stores for their school outfits and casual clothes, and then the boys would show up at around 3:00 and everybody would walk around. Sometimes they'd meet in Bresler's 33 Flavors for ice cream, giggles, gossip and even to share some of those transcendent adolescent moments when they tried to figure out parents, and teachers and God (if any).–William Severini Kowniski. (1978). The malling of America. New Times.

the number of women working outside the home. The percentage of nuclear families declined with people choosing to live alone, live together without marriage or live with friends and co-workers.

The increase in the numbers of women entering the workplace was significant. Divorced mothers worked to support themselves and their children. In addition, many wives from intact families also worked because of economic necessity or because they wished to add to the family income to achieve a better standard of living. By 1980, more than half of all women were working; by 1987, 55 percent of mothers of children under 6 were employed (Hymes, 1991). The total number of working women reached 54,742,000 in 1988 (Children's Defense Fund, 1990).

Another demographic change that affected childhood was the increasing proportion of people over 65. The increased life expectancy, combined with a lower birth rate, increased the percentage of the overall population who were living beyond age 75. Older citizens drained some of the nation's resources through Social Security payments, Medicare and disability payments. Families experienced additional stress as parents of dependent children were also taking responsibility for aging parents who depended upon them to provide for their physical and economic needs.

Family Lifestyle Changes

Personal fulfillment for adults became fashionable. It was acceptable to want to be successful, both professionally and personally. During the 1970s, the term "Me Generation" was used to describe the lifestyle that emphasized personal consumption, entertainment and fulfillment. A major religious revival in the 1970s included an interest in religious cults and trends such as Transcendental Meditation, Zen and evangelical Christian denominations. Religious enthusiasm was reflected in television evangelism, establishment of religious schools for children and activism by religious groups in public policy. The Moral Majority, founded in 1979, tried to influence political issues such as abortion and school prayer (Garraty, 1983).

The "Me Generation" was replaced by "Yuppies"

(young urban professionals) in the 1980s who were interested in the latest electronic gadgets, healthful food and fitness through jogging and other athletic activities. Fitness centers, offering a variety of exercise options, were complemented by tanning salons and fitness videotapes. Weight-loss fads were supported with diet books, weight-loss centers and new food products with lowered fat and calories.

By the end of the 1980s, the focus on personal needs and enjoyment was modified. Altruism and participation in global issues, such as environmental protection, caused personal consumption to become less fashionable. Interest in health continued, but the focus shifted to prevention of health problems and awareness of cholesterol in the diet rather than extremes in weight loss. The interest in religious movements was damaged by a series of scandals by televangelists that included marital infidelity, pornography and misuse of funds solicited from television audiences.

The family lifestyle was also affected by the large percentage of working mothers and single-parent families headed by both men and women. Family meals at home were replaced by eating out at restaurants and fast-food enterprises. This growing practice gave rise to concerns about children's nutrition. Advances in electronics made it possible for families to record and play their own videotapes, or rent videotaped movies for family viewing at home. The videotape recorder became as necessary as the television set had been in earlier decades. Family recreation increasingly centered on rented movie videotapes and cable television that allowed the family choices of a broad variety of programming, from educational shows to adult movies. Electronic games and personal computers provided additional sources of entertainment and recreation within the home.

In both nuclear and single-parent families, weekends were used for completing household tasks, home maintenance and shopping combined with family recreation. Children might spend much of the weekend in the family automobile while parents ran errands or shopped. The shopping mall increased in popularity as a social event, in addition to being a commercial resource for purchases, dining and browsing.

Conditions of Childhood: A Period of Change
The role of children in the family was altered to fit the new family lifestyle. Increasing numbers of children had to adjust to divorce that meant living with a single parent and, in many situations, reduced economic circumstances. Children from divorced families also had to learn to accept the loss of the noncustodial parent and adjust to the advent of a stepparent and many combinations of blended families

WINDOW TO THE WORLD
If the national news in the United States is concerned mainly with national and world stories and the drama violence of international relations, the local news—such a staple of the television scene in the U. S., where television service is far more decentralized than in most other Western nations—deals mainly with crime and violence on the local level, in much the same fashion, with the more dramatic and sensational stories occupying the foreground. The local news programs, because they are concerned with a smaller geographic area and relatively more mundane material, have become increasingly preoccupied with entertaining their audiences with amusing and titillating features. On an uneventful day with little important news, items have to be invented or created. The local anchormen and anchorwomen take the opportunity to groom their well-loved personalities and cultivate their audience allegiance.–Martin Esslin. (1988). Window to the world. In T. J. Crimmins & N. L. Shumsky (Eds.), *American life, American people, Vol. II* (p. 251). San Diego: Harcourt Brace Jovanovich.

with step-siblings and half-siblings (Coleman, Ganong & Henry, 1984; Skeen, Robinson & Flake-Hobson, 1984; Wallerstein, 1989). The reality of new family structures, along with the adjustments to new living situations, different schools and an unfamiliar role as the child of divorced parents, put many of these children at risk.

Children of the "Me Generation" were more likely to be in day care or unsupervised after school if they were of school age. Parents needing care for the children were faced with the difficult task of finding quality care for their preschool children, as well as temporary alternative care when their children experienced an illness. In 1979, the Children's Defense Fund reported that licensed day care slots were available for only 10 percent of the children of working mothers needing daily care. School-age children, who were under self-care, came to be known as "latchkey" children because they usually wore the key to their home around their neck.

Children of the 1970s had to accommodate to the fast pace of change in their lives. Access to television and its homogenizing effect on the population gave children constant access to changing current events of a global nature. They were part of a rushed society that expected them to take more responsibility and mature quickly (Bain, 1981). Neil Postman (1982) and David Elkind (1981) characterized the condition as a loss of childhood. Children were expected to dress, behave and learn in a precocious manner that put them under stress. Elkind characterized children in the 1970s as "hurried" because they were expected to help their parents adjust to the daily stress caused by the demographic changes especially prevalent during that decade.

Children of the 1980s, growing during the "Yuppie" period, were exposed to different stressors. Yuppie parents, unlike parents in the 1970s, were described by Elkind (1987) as being more in charge of their lives. These parents were competitive in their approach to their children's upbringing. Children in the 1980s were pushed and overprogrammed because their parents wanted "superkids" who would excel. They were pressured and at risk because parents, society and school expected them to learn more at a faster rate, in competition with children in their own culture as well as those in other countries.

Children and Television. A Growing Influence. By 1975, television sets were available to the majority of children in the United States. As programming for children expanded, there was a growing concern for the quality of shows targeted for child audiences. In 1968, Action for Children's Television was organized to advocate for appropriate television programming for children. Throughout the 1970s, ACT and other groups pressured for federal regulations of commercials aimed at children. The concern was over advertising of foods with a high sugar content and toys with questionable play value (Hymes, 1991).

Shows depicting violence were another concern. Some of the programs were not designed for children, but likely to viewed by the whole family. Violent cartoons developed for children were also targeted. In 1982, 3,000 studies documented the effect of television violence on children. Despite this information, the studies had little effect on improving television programming for children. In 1985, ACT submitted an official complaint to the Federal Communications Commission because programs were being developed around the toys advertised on television (Hymes, 1991). In 1991, these programs continued, especially on Saturday morning time periods.

On the positive side, there were excellent programs for children on television, among them *Captain Kangaroo, Mister Rogers Neighborhood* and *Sesame Street.* Unfortunately, *Captain Kangaroo* was cancelled by CBS but later reappeared on public television through the Corporation for Public Broadcasting. Public television continued its commitment to *Sesame Street* and *Mr. Rogers* and added *Villa Allegre, Bilingual Children's Television* in 1974.

Despite many efforts to improve television programming and commercials, little progress was made in convincing the major networks to improve their offerings for children. In the late 1980s, cable networks began to offer parents a broader selection for children through channels such as the Discovery Channel and Arts and Entertainment Network. Unfortunately, children who had access to cable networks could also watch MTV broadcasts of popular music with questionable visuals. In addition, adult movies and programming that stressed violence were accessible to children on cable networks.

Improvements in Child Health and Safety. Advances in treatment of childhood diseases successfully reduced or improved children's chances of survival. In 1977, a new vaccine, effective against a form of pneumonia that affected Black children with sickle cell anemia, improved that population's chances of battling the disease. Advances in the treatment of a childhood leukemia, lymphoblastic leukemia, led to longer periods of remission. The 10th anniversary of the last case

of smallpox was celebrated in 1987, as well as a successful heart transplant in a neonate and the transplant of five key organs in a 3-year-old child. A year later, a dramatic drop in dental cavities and decay was announced, attributed to the widespread use of fluoride. The announcement reported that nearly 50 percent of American children, ages 5 to 17, had no tooth decay. In 1989, a new test for genetic defects, chorionic villus sampling, was announced. The test, which could be done as early as eight weeks after conception, reassured many women at risk of having children with birth defects that the developing fetus was normal.

Other health improvements included development of a vaccine against bacterial meningitis and the discovery that aspirin given to children for flu or chicken pox could cause Reye's Syndrome. The Office of Health and Human Services issued a regulation in 1986 requiring the aspirin industry to print a label warning. The Environmental Protection Agency required the nation's refineries to take 91 percent of the lead out of gasoline by January 1, 1986, estimating that the action would halve the number who would suffer from lead poisoning.

Advances were also made in child safety between 1975 and 1992. The Consumer Product Safety Commission issued a regulation setting the minimum size for baby rattles and banned Tris, a fire retardant used in the manufacture of children's nightwear, which was found to cause cancer in test animals. Research commenced on a different chemical that would protect children from flammable nightwear. Childproof packaging on insecticides and medicines reduced the incidence of child poisoning. A 90 percent reduction of child poisoning in 1986 was attributed to child-resistant packaging, parent alertness and the contribution of 319 poison control centers throughout the United States.

More children were dying from automobile accidents than disease. According to the Academy of Pediatrics in 1981, nearly 1,000 children between birth and age 5 were killed and 60,000 injured each year. A campaign to promote the proper use of seat belts was initiated. In 1982, states began to mandate the use of safety seats for children under 5; by 1983, 41 states had passed safety seat legislation (Hymes, 1991).

In spite of improvements in health care and safety, the nation's children were at risk because of new health and safety risks and setbacks in some areas of prevention. Among these new concerns were the decline in immunizations, the spread of AIDS, health and safety problems in the expanding day care industry and babies at risk from mothers addicted to drugs and alcohol.

Although immunizations had been available to protect infants and children from childhood diseases for many decades, many children still were not immunized in the 1970s. In 1977, the Centers for Disease Control estimated 20 million children under the age of 15 were not fully immunized. The Department of Health, Education and Welfare funded $23 million in a National Immunization Initiative to immunize 90 percent of all children by 1979. The goal was met for school-age children; however, another goal had to be set for preschool children that was never met. In 1982, measles had almost been eliminated. Unfortunately, a measles outbreak in 1986 was attributed to unvaccinated preschoolers. Measles claimed the lives of 3,500 children in a further decline in the numbers of children immunized against measles, polio, rubella, diphtheria, pertussin and tetanus. Loss of federal funding and the rising cost of vaccine were blamed for the spreading problem. In 1990, measles outbreaks occurred in 25 states; health officials predicted an epidemic with 25,000 cases expected that year (Hymes, 1991).

A major health problem affecting children in growing numbers after 1975 was AIDS (Acquired Immune Deficiency Syndrome). In 1986, the spread of AIDS to children through blood transfusions and birth to an infected mother had reached epidemic proportions (Fetter, 1989). In 1987, HIV infections were reported in nearly 2,000 children. Although only 447 cases were reported in ages 0 to 5, 1,200 cases of AIDS were reported in 3- to 21-year-olds. By May 1988, 804 cases of AIDS were reported in children under the age of 5, making it the ninth leading cause of death among 1- to 4-year-old children. The Centers for Disease Control predicted that 3,000 infants would be born each year already infected with the AIDS virus (Children's Defense Fund, 1990).

Many of the babies born with AIDS had mothers who were also addicted to drugs. AIDS had been transmitted through shared needles among drug users. Children born to mothers who used drugs during pregnancy became a major problem in the 1980s. An estimated 375,000 babies were born to mothers in 1989 who used crack cocaine. In addition, use of alcohol during pregnancy was found to be a cause of physical and mental problems in children (Fury, 1982). An estimated 50,000 FAS babies were born each year with Fetal Alcohol Syndrome, accounting for approximately 20 percent of all cases of mental retardation (Schickedanz, Hansen & Forsyth, 1990).

The increase in the number of children in caregiving settings during this period gave rise to additional health and safety problems. Illnesses transmitted in child care were attributed to poor sanitary standards. In 1989, the American Public Health Association found a wide variation in health and safety standards among states. Handwashing procedures to control infectious diseases were required in less than half of the states. Sanitary food handling was required in 54 percent, and only 20 percent required energy-absorbing surfaces under playground equipment. In some centers, play equipment was improperly designed and installed. Other problems included equipment in poor repair or inappropriate for the size and age of the children (Wortham & Frost, 1990).

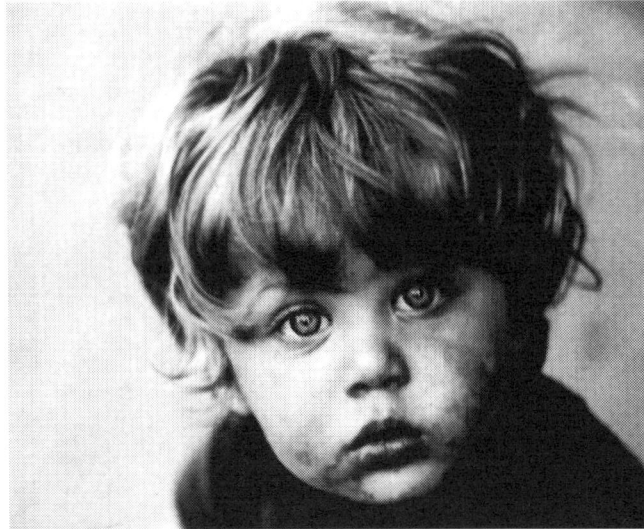

Awareness of the lasting effects of child abuse rose along with the number of cases reported. Campaigns aimed to build awareness of the problem were initiated on television by the National Committee on Child Abuse and the Advertising Council in1976. The number of reported cases and suspected unreported cases of abuse and neglect rose continually throughout the period. In 1977, it was estimated that 5 million children had been punished by their parents with violence that included being shot, stabbed, kicked and beaten. Child abuse was most likely to occur when families were under economic stress, when the parents had been abused as children and when a single parent, usually the mother, had most of the responsibility for raising the children. According to the Children's Defense Fund (1990), crack cocaine use accounted for a tripling of the number of New York City cases, between 1986 and 1988, in which parents neglected or abused their children. Drugs and alcohol accounted for more than half of the nearly 6,000 abuse or neglect cases reported in the District of Columbia between October 1988 and May 1990.

Child abuse, including sexual abuse, was also reported in child care centers in many states by 1984. Accurate information on child abuse in child care settings was difficult to document because of media exaggerations of reported cases and concerns for the accuracy of children's testimony in many of the cases that were brought to trial.

In spite of child abuse prevention programs and programs to rehabilitate children (Gunsberg, 1989) and parents who abused their children, the problem continued to grow (Finkelhor, 1984; Leavitt, 1981). In 1990, there was little indication that attempted solutions to child abuse and neglect were lowering statistics of abused children. Because of a shortage of child protection workers and services, little or no help was available to children who were known to be or suspected of being abused or neglected (Children's Defense Fund, 1990).

Changes in Public Attitudes Toward Children. In the 1950s and 1960s, healthy social and economic conditions were reflected in positive views of children. Programs of the Great Society, such as school lunch and breakfast programs, expansion of Aid to Families with Dependent Children and Medicaid, were based on a willingness to invest in children and optimism for their future. By the 1970s, the economic downturn and apparently insoluble economic problems resulted in a more pessimistic view toward investing in children. This changing attitude was bolstered by the initial findings of the Westinghouse study of the Head Start program that reported less success than had been hoped for.

Inflation, unemployment and the rising cost of living led to public resistance to funding programs for children. Taxpayer revolts against the rising costs of schooling and other areas of public spending were common occurrences in various cities and states. The defeat of Proposition 13 in California and reduced property taxes affected expenditures for parks and recreation programs, day care, welfare and educational programs. At the federal level, lowered expenditures at the end of the 1970s and throughout the 1980s drastically reduced funds for nutrition, child health care and social services. The negative attitude toward supporting the potential development of children generated an emphasis on custodial care for children rather than quality programming. Rehabilitation programs for troubled youth were replaced with institutions of incarceration. Compensatory education programs were reduced to restrictive levels of funding, while federal programs for college scholarships and loans were also cut or severely reduced. Public pessimism about the nation's economic future contributed to the decline of programs that would benefit children, particularly children of the poor.

Conditions for Poor and Minority Children

Poor and minority children were the hardest hit by reduced funding aimed at providing support services. The gains in reducing infant mortality, providing health care and reducing school dropouts that were achieved in the 1960s and the first half of the 1970s were lost in the 1980s. The gap between rich and poor widened in the 1980s, when more than 2 million children fell into poverty (Children's Defense Fund, 1990).

Decline in Federal Funding for Social Services. Poverty was widespread in the 1970s. By federal standards, 15.7 percent of children were considered to be in poverty in 1978 (U.S. Bureau of the Census, 1980). The Carnegie Council on Children (Keniston & Carnegie Council on Children, 1977) proposed that a quarter to a third of all American children were in families experiencing financial stress. In a recession period compounded by high inflation, even in families that had a parent who was employed, low wages kept the family at the poverty level. These families became known as the "working poor" (Children's Defense Fund, 1990).

The unemployed and working poor were further reduced to a situation of loss of self-respect because of public attitude. It was a period of crisis when the public had turned away from accepting responsibility for the needs of the poor. Instead,

the poor were held responsible for being poor and for the deterioration of their family. Children who were assisted by public programs had a stigma attached to them because their parents were considered to be inadequate and responsible for their child's condition. The prevailing attitude was that programs funded with federal money should pass cost-benefit criteria to ensure that the programs would pay off in future benefits from the money invested (Grubb & Lazerson, 1988).

A major target of the negative attitude toward funding programs for the poor was Aid to Families with Dependent Children. The basic income support program was criticized because it was funding families who were considered to be undeserving. Benefit cuts to this and other programs that included nutrition, child health care and other social services pushed many more children below or marginally above the poverty level. Cuts were made in food stamp and school lunch programs, Medicaid, and the Women, Infants and Children (WIC) program of nutritional supplements to pregnant and lactating women and infants. Each of these programs reached a dwindling number of children and families. For example, the AFDC program reached 83 percent of poor children in 1973; by 1987, only 59.8 percent of poor children were being served (Children's Defense Fund, 1990).

Isolation of the Poor. Because of declining sympathy with the circumstances of families in poverty, the poor became more isolated (Keniston, 1975). In addition, the nature of employment available to low-income workers was likely to be part-time, temporary and service sector jobs. The demographic information on the types of workers who fall into these categories lists young workers, the working poor, female-headed families, teen parents and minorities. Although President Reagan proposed that a "safety net" was in place to protect the deserving poor, in reality reduced funding of programs drastically cut the number of children needing assistance who could be served. As a result, children who were minority poor became more isolated from mainstream society. They were more likely to be homeless, live in a dangerous area, be under foster care and have health problems.

Homeless Poor. A phenomenon of the 1980s was homeless children. Low-income families were more likely to be unable to find affordable housing. Families depending on part-time or temporary jobs frequently faced the threat of becoming homeless. Because almost half of all poor renter households spent more than 70 percent of their income for housing, families with unstable incomes were frequently at risk for becoming homeless temporarily or for a longer period of time. The federal government's 80 percent cut in funding for low-cost housing found more families seeking temporary shelter. The average length of time to wait for assisted housing was 18 months. Families were often turned away from shelters for lack of space, or forced to split up to find shelter for part of the family at different locations (Children's Defense Fund, 1990).

Foster Care and Other Out-of-Home Placements. The numbers of children in foster care or other out-of-home care rose during the years between 1975 and 1990. While child neglect and abuse were factors, conditions such as homelessness and drug-related family problems also contributed to the rapid increase. By 1995, an estimated 840,000 children may be in foster care or emergency shelter care. Since 1985, New York City children entering foster care increased by 40 percent because of homeless-ness, unemployment, child abuse and neglect and lack of services for a parent needing treatment for drug abuse.

There was also an increase in young people placed in juvenile justice facilities. In 1986, more than 700,000 youths were being held for property crimes, alcohol and drug offenses, public order offenses and probation violation offenses. Some children detained in juvenile justice facilities had not been charged with any offenses. Emergency shelters, meant to be for short-term placement, became a dumping ground for children who could not be placed in foster care or other long-term placements. Infants born to mothers addicted to alcohol or drugs remained for months in hospital wards or emergency shelters when they were abandoned or removed from their mother's custody (Children's Defense Fund, 1990).

Urban Poor: Violence and Drugs. The high crime rates in inner-city neighborhoods made safety an issue for many urban poor and minority children. Because supervised programs outside school hours were not available to inner-city children, it was necessary for these children to remain in their homes to avoid the dangers in the streets. In Chicago, a survey of 536 elementary school children revealed that 26 percent had seen someone shot and 29 percent had seen someone stabbed. Approximately 12 million poverty children lived in violent, inner-city ghettos in the United States. They had to learn the rules of survival both within the home and on the streets. They were likely to be hyperactive or suffer from stress-related ailments, while their mothers were frequently clinically depressed (Children's Defense Fund, 1990; Kantrowitz, 1991). Zinmeister (1990) described the problem:

In May of 1987 the Mayor of Washington, D.C. visited an eighth-grade science class for gifted students at a public school in a poor neighborhood. The mayor posed a question. "How many of you know somebody who's been killed?" There were nineteen students in the class. Fourteen hands went up. The mayor went around the room: How were they killed? The answers began like this: "Shot." "Stabbing." "Shot." "Shot." "Drugs." "Shot." These were thirteen-year-old children. Given that they were in the gifted class, one can assume that they were from more privileged backgrounds than most of their schoolmates.

Over a four-month period in Detroit at about the same time, 102 youngsters age

sixteen or under were shot, nearly all of them by other children. There was so much violence in the public schools that the whole system had to be shut down for two days. (p. 50)

Health Needs of the Poor. While the average American child is healthy, poor children have health needs that have not been met. In the two decades prior to 1992, poverty children were more likely to be born to a teen mother, or to a mother who had not had prenatal care. The baby was more likely to be of low birth weight or die as an infant. During childhood years, poor and minority children were less likely to have received immunizations for measles, mumps and pertussis and more likely to have been exposed to lead poisoning. These conditions were a risk factor for school absenteeism, behavioral problems, poor coordination and dropping out of school. Poverty children were less likely to have health insurance and more likely to have decayed, filled and missing teeth. Native American, Black, Latino and migrant children were more likely to have dental disease that had not been treated.

Homeless children experienced special health problems. Shelters for the homeless were likely to have inadequate heating and ventilation, unguarded stairs and exposed electrical wiring. Because shelters were generally located in older buildings, children were likely to be exposed to lead paint. Diseases were regularly transmitted. Children were more likely to be behind in their immunizations because of their transient condition, and it was harder for them to recover from an illness when housed in a shelter.

Homeless children were more likely to be hungry and have poor nutrition. All members of a homeless family were at risk for becoming depressed or anxious because of the instability in their lives. Parents frequently were frustrated from loss of control for decision-making over their children because of shelter rules; and children were devastated by the loss or absence of toys and possessions that provided security. Family separations, caused by difficulties in securing housing or shelter, added to insecurity and instability. Going to school regularly was a problem; therefore, homeless children were more likely to have poor attendance and poor achievement in school (Children's Defense Fund, 1990; Eddowes & Hranitz, 1989).

CHILDHOOD EDUCATION: COPING WITH STRAINED RESOURCES AND CRITICISMS

The field of education suffered from the same limitations in 1975 as other programs in the United States. After a period of optimism about the promise of education to solve the nation's problems regarding poverty, disappointment in its failure manifested itself in the resources available to continue to improve education. Reduced funding for all levels of education and types of educational programs left the schools with tightened budgets and no longer able to meet the needs of diverse populations of students (Caldwell, 1982).

City schools were attended mostly by poor and minority students. Continued suburban development drained the schools of middle-class and upper-class students, minority as well as Anglo, as families who were able escaped deteriorating inner cities and overcrowded schools (Garraty, 1983). Increasing bureaucratization of schools resulted in a higher proportion of administrators as compared to teachers, with decisions about curriculum and instruction becoming the responsibility of the administrators, rather than the teachers. Teachers found themselves more limited in their professional opportunity to determine the best way to structure learning in their classroom. John Goodlad compared the current trend toward bureaucratization to his own years of schooling:

> From the perspective of distance, one of the most significant changes to take place within the educational system over the past four to five decades is bureaucratization. There was no superintendent and no central staff in the district where I went to school; nor did such exist in the larger district where I later taught. In the latter, the board hired (largely on the basis of an interview, with many candidates for each position) and fired (largely on the basis of an annual report on each teacher by the provincial school inspector). The secretary of the board (not an educator usually), commonly only employed part-time, saw to it that the few textbooks and essential materials were parcelled out to each school in a roughly equitable way. Principals taught and therefore were "inspected" as teachers; their administrative abilities included "discipline" and were judged largely on hearsay. Each school was, virtually by the facts of circumstances, a tub on its own bottom. (1988, p. 48)

The continuing trend toward centralization was also evidenced at the state level as state departments of education extended their authority and influence on what would be taught in the schools. As the numbers of children served by the public schools continued to rise, schooling became standardized to deliver an effective basic education.

The public perception was that the schools had failed. Teachers were responsible for the failure; therefore, they needed direction and supervision if children were to learn efficiently and become literate. The goal of the Great Society to eliminate poverty through education was unrealistic from its inception. The schools were never in a position to cure the social causes of poverty in the United States. The large amounts of money invested in schooling through compensatory education and early intervention programs had not eliminated the achievement differences between affluent and poor and minority students. Instead of evaluating how realistic the expectations of schools had been, the public held educators responsible for failing to achieve the desired results.

Effects of Civil Rights Efforts on School Achievement

The expectation that schools would not be able to achieve equity in education for all children came as early as 1966. It had been assumed that integration of schools and increased federal funding would be enough to equalize education of majority and minority children. The Coleman Report (Coleman et al., 1966), commissioned to determine if racial and ethnic groups were segregated from one another and whether schools offered equal educational opportunity, found that the great majority of American children attended segregated schools. Moreover, the academic achievement of minority students was one or two years behind White students in 1st grade. By the 12th grade, the disparity was three to five years (Coleman et al., 1966; Cremin, 1988). In 1965, President Johnson asked the Civil Rights Commission to collect information on racial isolation in the schools (Racial Isolation in the Public Schools, 1967). The report documented the inequalities of schooling for minority children in spite of integration. Despite integration, large numbers of minority children were still in racially isolated schools.

The disparity between schooling for White students and Black students confirmed the findings of the Coleman Report on achievement differences. The Civil Rights Commission recommended that action be taken to eliminate racial isolation in the schools. An affirmative policy to integrate schools was achieved through busing of students, following a series of court cases. The extent of busing to achieve integration was later modified in the Nixon administration and further questioned during Reagan's presidency in the 1980s. Massive demographic problems in achieving integrated schools in some heavily minority school districts, plus lack of confidence in the schools' ability to improve achievement through compensatory education, led to a focus on educating the individual student rather than busing to achieve racial integration (Cremin, 1988).

By the late 1970s, efforts to achieve equity in schooling were losing support. In spite of all the efforts in compensatory education, the disparity between minority and White achievement continued through the 1980s. There was less interest on the part of educators to provide pedagogy suited to the needs of minority children. It was common for teachers to label minority children as less able to learn and to identify family background as the cause of poor achievement. The family was to blame for the child's poor performance rather than the school. The belief of minority parents that education was the path to upward mobility was countered by educational practices that still perceived the potential of White children as more positive than that of minority children (Grubb & Lazerson, 1988). Public education had failed to achieve equal educational opportunity for all students and differences in class and race were still a consideration in the education of the nation's children. Children of the affluent received the best instruction and the best grades, while minority children often attended less well funded schools with inexperienced or less qualified teachers (Grubb & Lazerson, 1988).

In the late 1980s, the disparity between minority and Anglo achievement continued. The achievement gap narrowed slightly during the decade, but less than it had in the 1960s and 1970s. Minority children were still at risk for learning as revealed by statistics comparing minority and White achievement (Chafel, 1990). Forty percent of minority young people were functionally illiterate, and a minority child was 2.3 times more likely to be labeled as educably mentally retarded than a White child (Special Report,1989). The disparity between minority and White achievement followed the same pattern of widening during the years of schooling. Although minority students entered school only slightly behind their White counterparts, by 3rd grade Blacks and Latinos lagged by six months. By 8th grade, they were two years behind and by 12th grade, 3 years behind (Children's Defense Fund, 1990).

The 1980s also represented a period of less investment in the public schools as the major source for education of the American student. Under Presidents Reagan and Bush, initiatives were taken to lessen the responsibility of the federal government for supporting the funding of education. At the state level, actions to equalize funding among school districts were fought by wealthy school districts that felt the need to protect the services they were able to provide their students who came from affluent families. In a different approach, the concept being proposed of giving parents tax vouchers and allowing them the choice of where their child would attend school further weakened the obligation of state and federal governments to adequately fund education for all schools. The possibility of using public funding for private education was also considered to be detrimental to public schools. The drain of funding from the public sector would cause further deterioration of public schools that would most likely be serving larger percentages of poor and minority children (Grubb & Lazerson, 1988).

Higher Education
The decades of the 1970s and 1980s differed for higher education. The 1970s were marked by expansion and growth, while the 1980s were years of budget cuts and financial restrictions. Federal investment in higher education decreased, and state budgets also reflected shrinking revenues and expanded demands for social services to replace funds formerly provided from federal sources.

The perception of productivity and success in higher education was positive in the 1970s. Colleges and universities enjoyed a period of growth, expanded program offerings and general public approval. Stratification occurred as colleges became universities and universities became systems with campuses at various locations. The unrest on college campuses generated by the Vietnam War was past,

and students focused on preparation for a profession that would bring financial and personal rewards. Enrollments grew the most in colleges of business, engineering and computer science as undergraduate students looked forward to employment in the most lucrative areas of the economy.

Cremin (1988) wrote that higher education performed relatively well during the 1970s by providing large numbers of graduates for agriculture, business, industry and government. Nobel prize winners and recipients of other awards in fine arts, science and engineering were educated in the nation's universities. Most southern institutions were in compliance with the nondiscrimination provisions of the Civil Rights Act of 1964, with the result that Blacks and members of other minority groups had more opportunity to attend institutions of higher education. Because of continuing suburbanization, however, there were demographic limitations on where minorities attended college. For the most part, minority students attended public junior and four-year colleges and, historically, Black institutions. Much of the increase in college enrollment was among working class and minority students. Community colleges with lower entrance requirements and more accessibility in urban areas tended to attract lower income and minority students.

Although there were some critics of higher education in the 1970s, there were graver concerns in the 1980s. As Japan, Germany and other technologically advanced countries began to surpass the United States in research, design and marketing, institutions of higher education came under attack for not producing the quality of graduates needed to conduct necessary research. At the same time, universities found themselves unable to maintain the level of commitment to technological and scientific advances because of loss of income from federal agencies and foundations. Poverty students found the opportunity for higher education more difficult to achieve as universities raised tuition to try to pay for rising costs of operation. After 1980, cuts in federal aid for these students further limited access to financial assistance for college expenses. By 1988, less than half the number of students received federally funded Pell Grants as compared to the number of students served in 1980 (Cutler, 1989).

Jobs were harder to find after graduation in the late 1980s. Students found stiff competition for positions in almost every field. Years of recession, accompanied by many failed banks and businesses, meant that employers had eliminated positions in their firms or were cutting costs by not filling vacant positions until the national economy improved. Moreover, a college degree did not automatically mean the new graduate was in an enhanced position for employment. Specificity of skills and experience were more important than a college degree in some positions.

Schools of education were specifically targeted for criticism as a reform movement in education, "Back to Basics," swept public education. Teacher education was criticized for not adequately preparing their students for the demands of the profession. The perceived lack of rigor and low standards of teacher preparation programs were blamed for lower student achievement in elementary and secondary education. In a national move to reform teacher education (Carnegie Forum on Education and the Economy, 1986; Goodlad, 1986; Holmes Group, 1986), colleges of education moved toward reorganization of curriculum; some were eliminated in several states. Minimum competencies were established and standardized tests administered to graduates of teacher education programs in an effort to assure professionalism and competence in new teachers entering the field.

Secondary Education

Secondary education was the first level to receive the attention of critics of the schools. Coleman (1966) had earlier characterized high school student bodies as valuing athletic prowess and sociability higher than academic achievement. Assessments of achievement in the 1970s and 1980s, indicating a decline in most subjects, tended to confirm that perception and caused national alarm. In international assessments, American students compared poorly with students in other countries, particularly in science and mathematics (Cremin, 1988). Findings that students entering higher education were less prepared than previously in basic literacy skills, combined with a pattern of lower scores on Scholastic Aptitude Tests, led to public pressures for higher standards of instruction at the secondary level of education.

The call for reform came through a report titled *A Nation at Risk* (National Commission on Excellence in Education, 1983) which targeted weaknesses in secondary education. The report received widespread analysis and interpretation in education journals and the media. State legislatures responded to these concerns about American secondary education by passing legislation to increase requirements for graduation; expand course requirements in mathematics, science and English; extend the length of the school year; tighten standards for grades and eliminate social promotion. Statewide standardized tests to compare achievement among schools and minimum competency tests for high school graduation became the common method to assure that instructional improvement was resulting in higher achievement.

Elementary Education

Instead, however, of searching for a vision of what education could become as we move nearer to the twenty-first century, the response to the growing concern about education in the 1980s has been toward a stricter regimen in the schools: more stringent adherence to age-grade standards, more use of tests, more conformity, and a longer school day. This is a reinforcement of old methods that never worked very well. Instead

of incorporating new insights into the learning process, drill and practice become ensconced methodology. But drill and practice without understanding never produced effective learning. The danger in turning back to old strategies is that the concern for dignity and social relationships will be sacrificed without any corresponding gain in cognitive skills.–Evelyn Weber. (1984). *Ideas influencing early childhood education* (p. 202). New York: Teachers College Press.

The "Back to Basics" reform movement was quickly extended to the elementary level of schooling. State education agencies implemented legislated reforms that encompassed both secondary and elementary schools. Control of the curriculum became even more centralized as state agencies mandated statewide curriculum objectives from preschool through the 12th grade. Statewide achievement tests based on the mandated curriculum objectives were administered at various grade levels in the elementary school, with much analysis of the strengths and weaknesses of instruction among the state's school districts. The state's achievement tests replaced other factors in decision-making about curriculum and instruction. Instruction focused on preparation for the tests, while the curriculum was designed with the test in mind. Administrator and teacher anxiety about test results was the motivating force for the direction of elementary education. Instruction based on individual needs gave way to group instruction in the basic skills. Standards for promotion were based on a more demanding curriculum. Higher retentions in grade school resulted in renewed problems, with students dropping out when they reached junior high or high school.

The role of the elementary teacher also changed. With a state-mandated curriculum evaluated by statewide achievement testing, teachers had less autonomy in determining how they would teach in the classroom. Teacher-directed instruction and drill became the norm. Outdoor play, the creative arts, social studies and science became secondary to the basics of reading, writing and mathematics. Teacher evaluation focused on successful scores on achievement testing, with teaching behaviors expected to facilitate the achievement of high test results. Creativity in teaching had less value than skillful teaching of reading and mathematics skills.

The tragedy of American education now is that it is on the bandwagon of "quick fixes." Education has traditionally emphasized the memorization of information that did not make much sense to the learner. Things have become worse in recent years because the great majority of educators are on the achievement-test bandwagon. Teachers and principals worry about test scores, and few stop to ask if the pressure to produce higher scores is good for children's development.

Test mania is a symptom of adult heteronomy. Troubled by newspapers' publication of test scores, school boards all over the country are ordering superintendents to produce scores that are above the national average. Superintendents pass the order down to principals, and principals in turn decree that teachers produce higher test scores. The fact is that, by definition, achievement tests are made so that half of the population necessarily have to be below the national average. – Constance Kamii. (1988). Autonomy or heteronomy: Our choices of goals. In G. F. Roberson & M. A. Johnson (Eds.), *Leaders in education* (pp. 103-104). Lanham, MD: University Press of America.

Education of the Handicapped

The Education for All Handicapped Children Act (PL 94-142), an amendment to PL 93-380, extended and amended the Elementary and Secondary Education Act of 1965. The years between 1975 and 1992 were important ones for schools implementing the policies required by the act. Because the law mandated a free and appropriate education for all handicapped children, state laws had to be passed to accommodate the requirements to be met by schools. School districts had to provide training for teachers, parents, diagnosticians, special education teachers and administrators in order to adopt policies and practices that were in compliance with the law and also consistent with practices in other communities.

The Act required that handicapped children be evaluated to diagnose their strengths and weaknesses prior to developing appropriate educational plans for them. The stage of identification and diagnosis culminated in an Individual Education Plan (IEP) that was a cooperative effort by teachers, parents, diagnosticians, psychologists, if appropriate, and in some cases the student. Because the law specified that the child was to be placed in the least restrictive environment, the plans made for the student also described the process whereby the student would be mainstreamed into a regular classroom environment and receive special instruction by special education personnel as appropriate.

Because handicapped children had been served in separate classrooms prior to 1975, the new law involved extensive adjustments by school personnel, particularly regular classroom teachers. Ongoing inservice training was conducted to help all teaching personnel understand their new roles in serving children with special needs; however, a common complaint from classroom teachers was that they felt inadequate and unprepared to serve both handicapped and normal children (Lundsteen & Tarrow, 1981). Special education teachers frequently voiced concern that they and their special needs children were not accepted in the school.

Important information about mainstreaming and developing Individual Education Plans was learned during the first years. How much to mainstream was a common problem, particularly in early childhood classrooms. There were cases where children still remained isolated for too much of the school day. In contrast,

mainstreaming occurred for an extensive period that was too long for some children. Emotionally disturbed children were very difficult to place and serve adequately because of the individual attention they needed. It was found that some handicapped children felt more secure and learned more in an environment separate from regular classrooms.

In the late 1980s, much had been accomplished in improving the education and social environment for children with special needs. A whole generation of students had gone through the public schools with mainstreamed classes. Children and teachers had become accustomed to making the necessary daily transitions between special services and regular classroom instruction. Curriculum for special needs children had been developed as well diagnostic and psychological tests for screening, identification and diagnosis (Buchoff, 1990; Patterson & Wright, 1990). There were still problems and adjustments to be made. Difficulty in financing enough personnel for screening and identification in some schools meant significant delays in reaching children with individual services. Some parents still viewed the program as a stigma on themselves and their child and refused to have their child screened for identification. Nevertheless, progress had been made, and education had been normalized to a great extent for special needs students.

In 1986, PL 99-457 amended the Education of the Handicapped Act and called for establishing comprehensive programs of early intervention services for handicapped infants and toddlers and their families. In addition, it strengthened the requirements for states to serve all handicapped children between the ages of 3 and 5.

EARLY CHILDHOOD EDUCATION: AN EXPANDING ECOSYSTEM

Between the years of 1975 and 1992, the field of early childhood education experienced continued growth and change. Grant and Eiden (1982) reported that, in 1980, 52.5 percent of 3- to 5-year-olds were in early childhood programs, while 84.7 percent of the 5-year-olds were in programs. In addition to growth in the numbers of children served in public school, child care and Head Start classrooms, each of these settings experienced many variations in the types of programs and services they offered. More recently, as the institutions and settings offering care and education for children under 8 have broadened, the kinds of programs they offer have begun to overlap. Mitchell (1989) proposed that the field of early childhood education has become an ecosystem with interacting components that must engage in cooperative planning so that all can utilize the strengths, ideas and practices that can be gained from each individual type of setting.

Because different early childhood programs may have a variety of labels, it is sometimes difficult to understand what the name means (Law, 1979). Thus, in child care there is center-based and home care or family day care. Child care may be sponsored by an employer and be called corporate child care or industrial child care. Child care may be provided by a hospital or specialize in drop-in care for children who only need occasional care. The military services provide child care for military service men and women and civil service staff employed at military bases. Care in the home may also be provided by a thriving nanny business.

In the public school domain, early childhood programs may include pre-kindergarten or 4-year-old programs through 2nd or 3rd grade. Early childhood classrooms may serve children with special needs at the preschool and primary level. A newer phenomenon of classes between kindergarten and 1st grade may be called transitional 1st grade. A nursery school program may be part of a university laboratory school, private preschool or church-related preschool or day care (Lawton, 1988; Morrison, 1988;).

Often the name of the setting does not accurately describe the program or services, but has been chosen because it is fashionable or thought to appeal to parents. Whatever the title or location, expansion of the early childhood ecosystem is based on three main sources: continuation of early intervention, expansion and extension of public school programs and continued growth of child care and private preschools. Within these sources of programs, funding may come from federal, state and local governmental agencies; private sources such as corporations or large companies; parents and public schools. Frequently funding comes from a combination of resources.

EFFECTS OF SCHOOL REFORM
The "school reform" effort of the 1980s was not dramatic enough or drastic enough to produce the kind of jump-start our schools and children need. Children's scores on achievement tests improved in the 1980s, but only a tiny bit. Schools were the beneficiaries of far more rhetoric than resources. Federal help for elementary and secondary education actually fell 22 percent from 1979 to 1988. While state spending on schools rose some in the 1980s, the fastest state budget growth by far—twice as fast as education in 1988—was for prisons. The United States student-to-teacher ratio was nineteenth in the world in 1986, tied with Malta and Kuwait and lagging behind Libya, East Germany, Lebanon and Cuba. Our children know less geography than children in Iran, less math than school children in Japan, and less science than school children in Spain. In international test of math skills, our most advanced twelfth-graders ranked next to last.—Marian Wright Edelman. (1990). *S. O. S. America! A Children's Defense budget* (p.9). Washington, DC: Children's Defense Fund.

Continuing Interest in Early Intervention

Head Start. Although funding for intervention and compensatory programs was reduced after 1975, early intervention remained an area of interest and promise. Longitudinal research indicated that children in such programs fared better than their peers who did not have these educational experiences. A major source for documentation of the success of early intervention programs was the study of the long-term effects of Head Start (Brown, 1985). The Consortium for Longitudinal Studies followed children from six research-based Head Start programs. It was found that these programs had lasting effects on school competence, student attitudes and family outcomes. Students performed better on tests of achievement and intelligence, experienced fewer retentions in grade and fewer referrals to special education (Lazar & Darlington, (1982). In addition, studies have reported that high quality comprehensive early-intervention programs

give evidence of reduced incidences of juvenile delinquency and teenage pregnancy; participants also were more likely to graduate from high school (Berutta-Clement, Schweinhart, Barnett, Epstein & Weikart, 1984). Not all research on the effects of Head Start were positive in the early years of the program, but these more recent studies done from a longitudinal perspective gave cause for optimism for early education.

On an even more optimistic note, it appears that Head Start programs have become more effective over time. Children who attended Head Start after 1970 made nearly twice the cognitive gain as reported for children who attended Head Start in the start-up years between 1965 and 1969 (Collins, 1983). Although only about 20 percent of the children needing Head Start were served each year, more children were included in the program in more recent years. In 1990, Head Start celebrated 25 years of programs for preschool children. It had changed from a program for 5-year-olds to serving mostly 4- and 3-year-olds. In 1990, it served 488,470 children, the largest number in 20 years (Hymes, 1991).

Extension and Expansion of Public School Programs. Public schools were also expanding their early childhood intervention programs after 1975. The first programs had been for preschool migrant children, bilingual students and handicapped children served in response to PL 94-142. As positive results were documented for later effects of early intervention, more programs were added for children younger than 5 years in a downward extension below kindergarten into preschool programs. Early childhood programs serving handicapped children from 3- to 5-year-old children were joined by programs for 4-year-olds who were at risk because of cognitive and language limitations. In these programs, public schools were serving a similar population as Head Start programs, thus picking up many of the young children who could not be included in Head Start (Morrison, 1988). A few states are now implementing or considering programs for 3-year-old children (Blank, 1985), believing that earlier intervention parallel to Head Start programs will enhance the opportunity for at-risk children to overcome language and cognitive limitations.

A controversial source for the expansion of early childhood programs has been the advent of pre-1st grade programs beyond kindergarten. Transitional classrooms providing a program between kindergarten and 1st grade have been a response to the increased academic expectations of the Back to Basics movement that has resulted in use of a more advanced curriculum in kindergarten and 1st grade. As states implemented educational reform at the primary grade level, higher numbers of children were not able to perform well in 1st grade. With the additional policy of tighter requirements for promotion, many of these children were being retained in 1st grade or kindergarten (Shepard & Smith, 1986, 1987, 1989). An increase in the numbers of children in early childhood programs is partially due to children being placed in transitional programs to prevent failure and to better prepare them for the primary grades.

Growth in Day Care and Private Preschools

The major growth in the numbers of children in early childhood programs since 1975 has come within child care and private preschools. This has been in response to the demands by families for care of children during the working day. Child care is provided by private entrepreneurs who have a for-profit motive, churches that lease church school space for a program or sponsor child care in conjunction with a religious preschool program, and state and local agencies that run day care for low-income families in a federally funded or partially supported program. Child care programs are also initiated by large companies, corporations and community organizations to assist employees and citizens in their search for quality care. Hospitals frequently provide child care services either on-site or near their facility to ease the child care problems of health-care workers who have alternating schedules on a 24-hour basis. Public schools have entered the child care arena as they provide care for infants and toddlers during the day and extended care before and after school for latchkey children in response to parental requests (Lawton, 1988; Stroman & Duff, 1982).

The early childhood ecosystem is composed of preschool and primary grade programs that have diverse histories and purposes. Today they have more similar missions, yet are still varied in their sources of funding, administration and agencies of accreditation and supervision. A major concern in all types of settings is to improve the quality of programming offered for children; however, past history and conflicting views of program purposes raise issues and difficulties that affect the kind of learning programs that can be implemented.

Issues Affecting Program Development in Early Childhood Education

Head Start models served as sources for early childhood program development for many years. Curriculum materials and adult training strategies benefitted all types of settings for young children, including the public schools. Between 1975 and 1990, information about early childhood development and learning gained from Head Start models underwent further evolution and revision. Pure theoretical approaches gave way to more eclectic program combinations. The advent of the Back to Basics movement brought pressures for more academic instruction at earlier ages. By 1990, theories of child development were in conflict with pedagogy being used in response to the reform movement. The conflicts arose from opposing views of development and learning, issues in curriculum and

instruction and concerns about preparation of teachers of young children.

Issues in Curriculum and Instruction. The academic approach versus a child-centered, developmental approach to schooling was a problem in elementary schools, particularly in the primary grades and in preschool classes. Expectations from the educational reform movement that caused pressures for academic, structured instruction were in conflict with psychological theories of learning that believed in the teacher's role to facilitate intrinsic learning abilities in the child based on considerations of child development (Manning & Manning, 1981)

Program development became a response to external demands. In the public schools, Arnold Gesell's maturational theory was again prominent as schools attempted to understand and respond to the effects of increased academic demands on young children in the primary grades. Perceived immaturity or lack of readiness seemed the logical explanation for the failure of many children to complete successfully 1st-grade work within the curriculum and for instructional changes of the school reform movement in the 1980s. Determining the readiness of the child rather than the quality and appropriateness of the curriculum for the child's level of development became the instructional approach in many schools (Charlesworth, 1985; Kamii, 1985). The conflict between developmentally appropriate, child-centered instruction and academically oriented instruction rallied the support of early childhood specialists and organizations.

External demands on public education resulted from perceptions that public schools were not educating students to be able to compete with students in other countries and engage in the more demanding university programs in mathematics and science. The school reform movement with increased academic demands, more testing and raised expectations for promotion affected elementary education down through the primary grades and kindergarten. The more difficult curriculum in kindergarten and primary grades came to be called the "push-down" curriculum because the pedagogy used with the academic curriculum was not appropriate for the developmental levels of young children in the early childhood years.

Parents also put pressure on the schools to accelerate the curriculum because of the experiences children were having in child care and preschool programs prior to entering the public schools. Middle-class parents also felt competitive about their child's academic success (Elkind, 1987) and communicated to teachers and school administrators their expectations that their child was ready for more advanced curriculum.

The increased achievement testing that accompanied school reform and higher academic standards also exerted new pressures in public schools. It appears that school content and readiness for the next grade, plus testing and evaluation with limited cognitive objectives, were now important considerations for curriculum development in early childhood classrooms.

Increased percentages of failures in the early grades, as a result of more demanding curriculum and instruction, led to more testing (Perrone, 1991). Schools implemented transitional classrooms for children who were at risk to fail

1st grade. Readiness and other types of tests were used to identify children who would benefit from placement in a transitional classroom rather than the regular grade. The value of using standardized readiness tests for identification and placement of children in transitional programs was controversial, as were the transitional programs themselves, because they were a form of retention (Freeman, 1990; Bredekamp & Shepard, 1989; Meisels, 1987).

At the present time, public schools are still struggling with the problems of what type of curriculum should be used as well as the role of early childhood programs within the public schools. The child-centered curriculum (Lay-Dopyera & Dopyera, 1990) is proposed by some, while the academic curriculum (Gersten & George, 1990) is supported by others. The purpose for kindergarten is also being questioned (Simmons & Brewer, 1985; Webster, 1984), and half-day versus full-day kindergartens are under consideration or being implemented (Gullo, 1990; Mindes, 1990). While some states have responded to the calls for developmentally appropriate practices in early childhood classrooms through the primary grades (Bredekamp, 1987), others have yet to recognize the issues that need to be addressed. Teachers express frustration at the academic curriculum they are required to use with young children. They understand the kinds of active and interactive experiences young children need at their stage of development. They feel they lack the authority and empowerment to make professional decisions for the types of learning activities they implement in their classroom (National Association of Early Childhood Specialists in State Departments of Education, 1987).

In the meantime, current trends in program development hold promise for the future as well as presage difficulties in acceptance and implementation. Some would propose that the elementary school must be restructured to accommodate the developmental needs of children in the early childhood years. Two models that have been suggested are the ungraded primary and the early childhood unit. The ungraded primary would eliminate grade delineations prior to the end of 3rd grade. Children's developmental progress would be the determining factor in instruction rather than the present graded curriculum. The early childhood unit is also proposed as a solution to the need for instruction geared to the developmental differences in the early learning years. Preschool programs would be organized with primary grades and located separately from intermediate grades in elementary school.

Current trends in early childhood curriculum support developmental continuity in learning. Integration rather than separation of content areas in curriculum is being proposed as a more meaningful approach to the cognitive strategies and developmental differences in young children (Katz & Chard, 1990; Krogh, 1990). Understanding the connections children must make between existing knowledge and new information and concepts is important in all content areas. Whole language and emergent literacy theories, for example, consider this integrative view of learning to use written language. Curriculum for the early childhood years

based on developmentally appropriate considerations is now being promoted (National Institute of Education, 1985; International Reading Association, 1985).

Issues in Child Care and Preschool Programs. The need for child care has expanded faster than the ability of policymakers to develop standards for settings that provide care. The federal government has continued to act with reluctance in an area considered to be the responsibility of the family (Goffin, 1990; Grubb & Lazerson, 1988). In addition, because of the varied and competing programs that provide care, there is no overall policy for child care. As a result, child care policy is in chaos. States vary widely in their standards for child care programs, while national standards have not been established. The cost of child care varies within and among states; moreover, cost of care is not an indicator of the quality of the program. The significance of the variation in child care standards in the United States is emphasized by the following information provided by the Children's Defense Fund (1990).

STATE CHILD CARE STANDARDS
- Twenty-two states permit five or more babies to be cared for in child care centers by a single staff member without an assistant, and at least 10 states permit family day care providers to care for five or more babies alone.
- Twenty-nine states and the District of Columbia do not guarantee that parents can drop in unannounced to their children's child care center.
- Twenty-one states and the District of Columbia do not require any form of training for family day care providers.
- Twenty-three states and the District of Columbia do not have specific requirements for ongoing training for staff employed in child care centers. (p. 42)

Finding quality care is but one issue facing parents. Affordability is a major concern, particularly for poverty parents. Parents on marginal incomes just above the poverty line often find it easier to live on welfare payments than to seek employment and pay for child care. Subsidized child care is available, but inadequate because of long waiting lists in many states (Children's Defense Fund, 1990). The rising demand for infant care also is difficult to meet. Higher percentages of working mothers are returning to work shortly after the birth of a child, and finding appropriate care for infants is difficult because it is not cost-effective. The low adult-to-child ratio needed for infant care makes it difficult for child care centers to offer this service to parents (Honig, 1990). In spite of these problems, centers are recognizing the need and enlarging their programs to include care and programming for infants (Cataldo, 1982).

Child care center directors and owners are in a constant quandary of how to provide quality care and meet costs of center management. Unfortunately, the low wages that must be paid to caregivers if the center is to be cost-effective result in a high turnover in personnel and uncertainty about the quality of training they bring to the job (Wingert & Kantrowitz, 1990). Ongoing or comprehensive training is difficult to plan with frequent changes in staff members, and maintaining good personnel through improved pay is difficult without losing control of the center's budget.

Current trends in child care and private preschool programs give cause for hope. Although there are no national standards for the child care industry, the National Association for the Education of Young Children addressed the issue of a standard with a Center Accreditation Project (CAP) whereby child care centers, private preschools and before- and after-school programs can undergo a voluntary accreditation process. The accreditation process includes interactions among staff and child interactions, curriculum, staff and parent interactions, administration, staff qualifications and development, staffing patterns, physical environment, health and safety, nutrition and food service and program evaluation (National Association for the Education of Young Children, no date). Child care center directors have provided accountability to parents for the quality of their program by conducting the accreditation process in their centers. As a result, it is possible to identify excellent programs in many communities. The process is voluntary, however, and because state standards are lacking, the majority of child care programs are poorly supervised or totally unsupervised. Referral services to accredited programs exist in many communities, but the final responsibility of locating quality care still rests with the parents (Clark-Stewart, 1982).

Continuing Issues in Childhood Education

Most of the concerns in early childhood education are not new, but continue to affect young children in the various components of the ecosystem. As the ecosystem continues to become interrelated and interdependent, identification and successful closure of problems will require cooperation and understanding rather than competition and separation.

Role of the Family. Since the 1960s, continued research and interest in the role of the family in the child's development and learning have reinforced the philosophy that the family has the greatest influence on the outcomes of childhood and achievement. The role of the family in child care and schooling continues to be of prime importance (Powell, 1989). The question of what that role should be continues to be an issue. Public schools have not always embraced parental involvement. Child care centers are sensitive to parental approval, but do not necessarily look to parents for establishing policies and program. The partnership among parents, school and community in children's education will continue to evolve as more is learned about the parental role in learning and how the school and community can work with parents and children to enhance the quality of education (Fuller, 1989; Hopman, 1989).

Parents are already demonstrating a changing perception of their significance in their children's education. A growing minority of families in the United States are engaging in homeschooling. Families of all income and education levels, in both urban and rural areas, are homeschoolers. Their reasons for choosing this type of education range from the parents' desire to be directly involved in their child's education to rejection of the values being taught in the public schools. Some parents choose to educate their children because of religious beliefs, while others seek to be closer to their children as a family unit. Although homeschooling was fought by states and school districts in the early 1980s, the practice exists in various forms in most states now.

There are specific issues surrounding homeschooling. The quality of the child's instruction is frequently questioned, as is the equivalence of homeschooling to public school education. Schools and parents both are concerned about how to evaluate the child's learning and who should determine the content of the curriculum. These and other issues will continue to be explored in the future as more parents decide on homeschooling their children in order to play a stronger role in their children's education.

Role of Play in Early Childhood Education. The role of play in kindergarten, nursery school and child care programs was of prime importance throughout the 1960s. With the advent of the Back to Basics movement, however, its significance in learning has been questioned. Public schools have eliminated or drastically reduced the time and opportunity for play in an academic atmosphere that does not recognize development of the whole child in the early childhood years (Frost, 1992). Outdoor play has been diminished in the lives of young children who live in a temperature-controlled environment and whose parents are afraid to have them play outside the home in a dangerous urban neighborhood.

Private preschools and child care settings are more likely to permit outdoor play, especially since many children are in care for extended periods each day. It would seem, however, that parents and early childhood education practitioners, in general, are more focused on cognitive learning and have less interest in the role of play in young children's development and learning. Early childhood specialists continue to address this concern which has programmatic ramifications for all early childhood settings. Play experts continue their research in the belief that play is an essential element in development and learning (Hughes, 1991; Johnson, Christie & Yawkey, 1987). Through play, children integrate physical, social, emotional, cognitive, language and imaginative experiences (Frost, 1992; Hughes, 1991; Tegano, Sawyers & Moran,1989).

Role of Technology in Childhood Education. Computers have become readily available to school programs since 1980. With decreasing cost and abundant software, they are available for children of all ages. Although there had been concern that use of computers would tend to make children social isolates, evidence points to cooperative and collaborative efforts in children's use of computers. The early concern that most software replicated programmed workbooks and did not facilitate divergent thinking has been ameliorated by availability of more varied and appropriate software. Children as young as 4 can learn to program using LOGO, and language skills can be enhanced by cooperative efforts in using software designed for young children (Kaden, 1990).

The type of computer experiences accessible to the majority of young students in public schools, however, may not fit the positive characteristics listed above. Software used in primary grades still tends to be programmed instruction or drill that fails to promote creative thinking and group effort. In many schools, computers are not available in individual classrooms; therefore, groups of children are taken to the computer room once or twice a week for structured lessons, limiting exploration and play with computers. The availability of computers in child care programs depends upon the financial situation of the center; computers are more apt to be found in centers serving middle- and upper-class children. This can be perceived as widening the gap in educational experiences for affluent and poverty children in early education programs.

Teacher Preparation. The preparation of teachers varies among programs in different states. Although most states require an undergraduate degree and completion of requirements for certification, the content and expectations of the programs differ. Beginning in the 1970s, there was pressure on colleges of education to increase the rigor of teacher preparation and emphasize the liberal arts rather than methodology. In addition, there has been a trend toward lengthening teacher education programs to five or six years in order to prepare more competent teachers (Holmes Group, 1986; Carnegie Forum on Education and the Economy, 1986). How these issues will be resolved remains to be seen (Barbour, 1990).

The child care sector and private preschools have different issues to consider in teacher preparation. Because of low salaries coupled with different standards and policies from state to state, there is no consensus as to the best ways to prepare early childhood teachers outside of public schools. Access to training is a common problem (Klass & Nall, 1989). Training expectations vary from none to a two-year program or the equivalent for private school Head Start teachers. Programs for teachers in these settings are available in community colleges. An alternative to programs in institutions of higher education is the Child Development Associate Program, based on observable competencies required for early childhood caregivers. The CDA program requires observation of the candidate, informal or formal education experiences and 640 hours of experience of working with children in lieu of classroom training. A local assessment team (LAT), including the candidate, a professional trainer and a parent/community representative, assesses the candidate's proficiency on the competencies (Perry, 1990).

Teacher preparation is further complicated by the diversity in the field. Bilingual education, multicultural education, early childhood programs for the handicapped and programs for gifted children are all part of childhood education programs. Training for teachers for each of these programs is different in some aspects. The generally low standards of training required in day care, Head Start and some private preschools imply that specializations within these programs for special needs children will continue to be a challenge within present training policies.

In the summer of 1991, approximately 75 graduate students from The University of North Texas, East Texas State University, Texas Women's University and The University of Texas at Arlington spent five days together in Dallas in a workshop focused on current trends and issues in early childhood and elementary

education. On the final day, participants were asked to comment on changes and issues that would continue into the beginning of the 21st century. Their responses reflected situational influences of the community and region in which they teach, as well as their own interests and values.

Some participants focused on changing demographics in student populations. They commented on the need for increased emphasis on education of minorities to respond to population shifts. The growing political influence of minority groups was predicted to be a factor in pressures for curriculum changes. Another factor was the perception that public schools will increasingly serve low-socioeconomic status students if the use of vouchers becomes actuality and more affluent parents move their children into private schools.

An increase in homeschooling was predicted as an alternative to public education. Parents who question the success of public education may be willing to use their own financial resources to secure a "better" education for their children.

Participants also addressed changes in teacher education. They expressed concerns that extending initial training of teachers into five-year programs would increase the cost of education and professional certification. Another related concern was a subsequent reduction in federal and state funding for teacher preparation programs.

Other changes predicted for schools and curriculum included the move to year-round schools. Some participants stated that, to meet families' increasing needs for a support system, schools may have to expand their programs and become centers for parent and family education, recreation, child care and health and social services.

The school curriculum will incorporate more use of personal computers. The continued decrease in the cost of laptop computers will eventually make them affordable for individual students. Financial resources may then be diverted to purchase and maintenance of computers as well as continual acquisition of newly developed software. Teachers will have to address the issues of education by computer, which will involve a changing teaching role, individual learning and social implications for the classroom.

Finally, participants predicted that the school curriculum will expand the emphasis on environmental protection and conservation. Not only will teachers become more involved as advocates and sources of information on environmental issues, but schools will have to become models for conservation and recycling if students are to commit their efforts to finding environmental solutions.

Only time will tell how well today's graduate students and practicing teachers can see into the future. One group of participants half-seriously considered the issues involved in schooling children living on space stations. This, too, is within the realm of possibility.

ACEI, PREPARING FOR THE FUTURE: 1975-1992

The years since 1975 have been difficult ones for ACEI. They have been years of change, decisions and relocation as the leadership and members sought to determine a niche for the organization in the face of declining membership. Executive Boards faced continuing challenges in an effort to find the direction for a smaller organization. Uncertainty reflected by cuts in the headquarters staff was aggravated by several changes in Executive Directors.

A significant activity to focus ACEI's mission was the adoption in1975 of a Plan of Action that provided a framework for branch efforts, publications and conference discussion topics. Task Forces addressed elements of the Plan of Action to develop and interpret the plan for the organization. Expansion in the scope of service to children, which now ranged from infancy through early adolescence as adopted in 1971, was also addressed through conference topics, publications and committee work.

Throughout this 27-year period, the shift from branch to individual memberships resulted in total membership decline. Efforts were made to determine the causes. A questionnaire sent to members and inactive members sought information as to why members became inactive. Responses revealed that the largest loss in membership was in members between the ages of 23 and 30. Members were mostly public school teachers who felt that the organization did not meet their specific interests or that they had no opportunity to get actively involved. This information was shared with branches to assist them in their efforts to recruit and retain members at the local level.

Sale of ACEI Childhood Education Center

In an effort to solve persisting financial problems, the 1982 Executive Board decided to sell the ACEI Childhood Education Center on Wisconsin Avenue. Two houses next to the center had been sold in 1978, but proceeds from their sale were not enough to stabilize finances. A buyer was found for the building in 1984 and a suite of offices subsequently located in Wheaton, Maryland, for headquarters staff. Sale of the building enabled the organization to pay off current debts and invest some of the proceeds for future use. In late 1991, offices were again relocated in Wheaton, Maryland , to better accommodations for the association's work.

The sale of the headquarters building was difficult, especially since it had been a great source of pride for members. Nevertheless, ACEI continued to focus on future possibilities for the organization rather than regrets for the necessary change.

Addressing Issues

One of ACEI's major contributions was its involvement in addressing current issues. In 1977, ACEI joined the National Association for the Education of Young Children, Association for Supervision and Curriculum Development, National Association of Elementary School Principals, National Council of Teachers of English and International Reading Association in issuing *A Joint Statement of Concerns About Present Practices in Pre-First Grade Reading Instruction*. The statement responded to the growing practice of stressing academic instruction with kindergarten children. In 1984, ACEI joined the U. S. Committee of OMEP and NAEYC in sponsoring five noncopyrighted articles that focused on the rights of children. Titled Reaffirmations: Speaking Out for Children, the series addressed the child's right to food, to play, to imagine, to learn and to the valuing of diversity.

ACEI also issued position papers on the expressive arts, corporal punishment, standardized testing, child-centered kindergartens and preparation of early childhood teachers. In 1988, two position papers were issued on play and the right to quality child care.

A Significant Role for ACEI Publications

Publications produced during this period also focused on issues in the field. Articles in *Childhood Education* addressed concerns of parents and educators, as did theme issues and special publications. ACEI publications continued to be a strength of the organization.

Childhood Education enjoyed recognition as an award-winning journal. In 1975, The Journal received the Education Press Association of America Distinguished Achievement Award for Excellence in Education Journalism. In 1979, it was awarded the Washington Education Press Association Eleanor Fishburn Award for Excellence in the Promotion of Human Understanding. Still other awards followed: 1983, National Association of State Education Department Information Officers, Award of Excellence in Education Communications; 1984, American Society of Association Executives, Gold Circle Award; 1986, National Association of State Education Department Information Officers, two Awards of Excellence in Education Communications; 1986, Washington Education Press Association, two Distinguished Achievement Awards; 1991, Washington Education Press Association, Excellence in Print Award.

ACEI's expanded mission to serve a wider range of ages in childhood was reflected in its first publications addressing infancy and early adolescence: *Understanding and Nurturing Infant Development* and *Early Adolescents: Understanding and Nurturing Their Development*. Other significant publications included *Dauntless Women in Childhood Education* and *Learning from the Inside Out: The Expressive Arts*. A major step forward was taken with initiation of the *Journal of Research in Childhood Education* in 1986. This new journal is focused on educational research related to children from infancy through early adolescence, providing a new service to members that differs from the theory-into-practice articles found in *Childhood Education*. In 1988, *Childhood Education* also appeared in a new, larger format with color featured on the cover. Division Newsletters focusing on different age groups served by ACEI were launched in1989 to address specific interests and concerns of members. In 1991, *Childhood Education* was further enhanced with the inclusion of color on inside pages and the return of *ACEI Exchange*. The most recent publications–*Readings from Childhood Education Volume II; Personalizing Care with Infants, Toddlers and Families*; and *Common Bonds: Anti-Bias Teaching in a Diverse Society*–rounded out the list of significant publications produced by the organization.

Celebrating a Centennial Year: Looking to the Future

By the end of the 1980s, ACEI entered a more optimistic time. Planning for ACEI's centennial celebration sparked new interest in the organization. Members looked forward to publication of *Profiles in Childhood Education 1931-1960*, a project of the Later Leaders Committee. A sequel to *Dauntless Women in Childhood Education 1856-1931*, the book is a collection of *Childhood Education* articles featuring the lifetime achievements of 26 ACEI leaders.

Other developments gave cause for optimism. There was a gradual rise in membership numbers. Attendance at annual conferences began to show a modest but significant increase. Marketing consultants assisted the organization in analyzing how to attract and retain new and former members.

In addition, the National Council for Accreditation of Teacher Education (NCATE) designated ACEI as the organization to conduct the accreditation process for elementary certification programs in colleges and universities providing teacher education. Accepting responsibility for the process, the Teacher Education Committee piloted an accreditation plan in 1990 and developed the 1992 ACEI

publication titled *Elementary Education Curriculum Folio Guidelines for the NCATE Review Process*. The first group of volunteer evaluators received training at the 1991 Study Conference in San Diego, California, and subsequently participated in the evaluation of portfolios that had been submitted to ACEI. This opportunity not only enlarged the possibility for service by the organization, but also the potential for increasing membership.

ACEI faced the centennial year with new hope. The organization sought to redefine its role in a new century, knowing that the concerns would be significantly different from those faced by "kindergarteners" in 1892. How the Executive Board, members and headquarters staff determined that role and opportunity would decide the direction and future history of an organization with a long and proud past.

In 1992, like 1892, there were many issues and opportunities available to members of the organization. A renewed interest in the early childhood years from birth to age 8 as critical years for development and learning, particularly for children at risk for successful schooling, resulted in funding for innovative programs in schools throughout the United States. Emphasis was placed on continuity in learning rather than differences between preschool and primary school. Child-centered methods such as cooperative learning and integrated instruction were encouraged for preschool and elementary grades at state and national levels of education. National and international attention was directed to the problems of successfully educating children from diverse backgrounds. Opportunities and challenges abounded as the organization faced a second hundred years and a new century. The future strength of the organization depended on how the organization interpreted its mission and how new members embraced its goals.

In 1985, a videotape about ACEI anticipated future challenges with these words:

> How will ACEI meet the challenges of the future? We are no longer an organization of the United States, but part of a global community. The world is no longer a collection of nations organized by hemisphere or opposing ideologies. As a global community, we affect and are affected by the advances and conditions encountered by each separate nation. Our world is beset with wars, famine and regional struggles for power and control. At the same time, technological advances are revolutionizing how we live, work and play. We are a global community with as many opportunities as problems. Change is rapid and pervasive. A key to the future is coping with change and using flexible problem-solving to improve the quality of life for children. (Wortham, 1985, p.78)

In 1992, this statement was still accurate. There were abundant challenges to be seized by the membership and leaders of ACEI. It was just a matter of determining how best to take action that would improve life and learning for children and their families in a new world full of possibilities as well as problems.

REFERENCES

Anderson, J. D. (1988). *The education of Blacks in the South, 1860-1935*. Chapel Hill: University of North Carolina Press.

Aries, P. (1962). *Centuries of childhood: A social history of family life* (R. Baldick, Trans.). New York: Vintage Books.

Association for Childhood Education. (1931, December). Minutes of Executive Board Meeting.

Association for Childhood Education. (1933, December). Minutes of Executive Board Meeting.

Association for Childhood Education. (1937). *The kindergarten centennial 1837-1937*. Washington, DC: Author.

Bain, W. E. (1967). *75 years of concerns for children*. Washington, DC: Association for Childhood Education International.

Bain, W. E. (1981). With life so long, why shorten childhood? In J. S. McKee (Ed.), *Early childhood education 83/84* (pp.27-29). Sluice Dock, CT: Dushkin Publishing Group.

Barbour, N. (1990). Issues in the preparation of early childhood teachers. In C. Seefeldt (Ed.), *Continuing issues in early childhood education* (pp. 153-171). Columbus, OH: Merrill.

Barrett, R., & Becker, P. (1933, June). Report to Exectuive Board. Washington, DC: Association for Childhood Education.

Beard, C. A., & Beard, M. (1944). *A basic history of the United States*. New York: Doubleday, Doran & Co.

Becker, P. (1933, December). Report to Executive Board. Washington, DC: Association for Childhood Education.

Bereiter, C., & Engelmann, S. (1973). Observations on the use of direct instruction with young disadvantaged children. In B. Spodek (Ed.), *Early childhood education* (pp 176-186). Englewood Cliffs, NJ: Prentice-Hall.

Berrueta-Clement, J.R., Schweinhart, L.J., Barrett, W.S., Epstein, A.S., & Weikart, D.P. (1984). *Changed lives: The effects of the Perry Preschool programs on youths through age 19*. Monographs of the High/Scope Educational Research Foundation, 8. Ypsilanti, MI: High/Scope Press.

Biber, B. (1973). Goals and methods in a preschool program for disadvantaged children. In B. Spodek (Ed.), *Early childhood education* (pp. 248-262). Englewood Cliffs, NJ: Prentice Hall.

Blank, H. (1985). Early childhood and the public schools. *Young Children, 37* (4), 52-55.

Bloom, B. (1964). *Stability and change in human characteristics*. New York: John Wiley.

Bonn, M. (1976). An American paradox. In E. H. Grotberg (Ed.), *200 years of children* (pp. 160-169). Washington, DC: U. S. Government Printing Office.

Boston Herald, Thursday April 24, 1902.

Braun, S. J., & Edwards, E. P. (1972). *History and theory of early childhood education*. Belmont, CA: Wadsworth.

Bredekamp, S. (Ed.). (1987). *Developmentally appropriate practice in early childhood programs serving children from birth through age 8*. Washington, DC: National Association for the Education of Young Children.

Bredekamp, S., & Shepard, S. (1989). How to best protect children from inappropriate school expectations, practices, and policies. *Young Children, 44* (3), 14-24.

Brown, B. (1985). Head Start: How research changed public policy. *Young Children, 40* (5), 9-13.

Buchoff, R. (1990). Attention deficit disorder: Help for the classroom teacher. *Childhood Education, 67*, 86-90.

Butler, A. L. (1991). Will Head Start be a false start? In J. D. Quisenberry, E.A. Eddowes & S. L. Robinson (Eds.), *Readings from Childhood Education Volume II* (pp.208-211). Wheaton, MD: Association for Childhood Education International.

Caldwell, B. M. (1982). Our children, our resources. *Childhood Education, 58*, 274-280.

Carnegie Forum on Education and the Economy. (1986). *A nation prepared: Teachers of the 21st century*. New York: Author.

Cataldo, C. Z. (1982). Very early childhood education for infants and toddlers. *Childhood Education, 58*, 149-154.

Chafel, J. A. (1990). Needed: A legislative agenda for children at risk. *Childhood Education, 66*, 241-242.

Charlesworth, R. (1985, Spring). Readiness: Should we make them ready or let them bloom? *Day Care and Early Education*, 25-27.

Children's Defense Fund (1990). *S. O. S. America! A Children's Defense budget*. Washington, DC: Author.

Clark-Stewart, A. (1982, September). The day care child. *Parents*, 72-75.

Coleman, J. S., Campbell, E. Q., Hobson, C. J., McPartland, J., Mood, A. M., Weinfeld, F. D., & York, R. L. (1966). *Equality of educational opportunity*. Washington, DC: U. S. Government Printing Office.

Coleman, M., Ganong, L. H., & Henry, J. (1984). What teachers should know about stepfamilies. *Childhood Education, 60*, 306-309.

Collins, R. (1983, Summer). Headstart: An update on program effects. *Newsletter of the Society for Research in Child Development, 2*.

Committee of Nineteen. (1913). *The kindergarten*. Boston: Houghton-Mifflin.

Consortium for Longitudinal Studies. (1983). Lasting effects of early education. *Monographs of the Society for Research in Child Development*.

Cooper, S. B. (1893). The kindergarten and its bearing on crime, pauperism, and insanity. In Committee on the History of Child Saving Work, *History of childsaving in the United States* (pp. 89-98). Boston: Geo H. Ellis.

Cremin, L. A. (1961). *The transformation of the school*. New York: Alfred A. Knopf.

Cremin, L. A. (1988). *American education*: The metropolitan experience 1876-1980. New York: Harper & Row.

Curti, M. (1971). *The social ideas of American educators*. Totowa, NJ: Littlefield, Adams & Co.

Cutler, B. (1989). Up the down staircase. *American Demographics, 11*, (4), 32-41.

Datta, L. (1976). Watchman, how is it with the child? In E. H. Grotberg (Ed.), *200 years of children* (pp. 221-279). Washington, DC: U. S. Government Printing Office.

Day, M. C., & Parker, R. K. (Eds.). (1977). *The preschool in action* (2nd ed.). Boston: Allyn & Bacon.

Deutsch, M. (1963). Nursery education: The influence of social programming on early development. *Journal of Nursery Education, 18*, 191-197.

Dewey, J. (1899). *School and society*. Chicago: University of Chicago Press.

Dewey, J. (1938). *Experience and education*. New York: Macmillan.

Dixon, G. (1990). The first years of kindergarten in Canada. Unpublished manuscript.

Eddowes, E. A., & Hranitz, J. L. (1989). Educating children of the homeless. *Childhood Education*, 65, 197-200.

Elkind, D. (1981). *The hurried child*. Reading, MA: Addison-Wesley.

Elkind, D. (1987). *Miseducation*. New York: Alfred A. Knopf.

Erikson, E. (1950). *Childhood and society*. New York: W. W. Norton.

Farmer, J. (1976). Toward equal educational opportunity. In E. H. Grotberg (Ed.), *200 years of children* (pp. 188-199). Washington, DC: U. S. Government Printing Office.

Fetter, M. P. (1989). AIDS education. Every teacher's responsibility. *Childhood Education*, 65, 150-153.

Finkelhor, D. (1984). The prevention of child sexual abuse: An overview of needs and problems. *SIECUS Report, XIII* (1), 1-5.

Frank, L. (1962). The beginnings of child development and family life: Education in the twentieth century. *Merrill-Palmer Quarterly, 8* (4), 7-28. Also cited in S. J. Braun & E. P. Edwards (1972), *History and theory of early childhood education*. Worthington, OH: Charles A. James.

Freeman, E.B. (1990). Issues in kindergarten policy and practice. *Young Children, 45* (4), 29-34.

Frost, J. L. (1992). *Play and playscapes*. Albany, NY: Delmar.

Frost, J. L., & Wortham, S. C. (1988). The evolution of American playgrounds. *Young Children, 43* (5), 19-28.

Fuller, M. L. (1989). Delayed parenting: Implications for schools. *Childhood Education*, 66, 10-107.

Fury, E. M. (1982). The effects of alcohol on the fetus. *Exceptional Children, 49*, 30-34.

Garraty, J.A. (1983). *A short history of the American nation*. New York: Harper & Row.

Gerston, R., & George, N. (1990). Teaching reading and mathematics to at-risk students: What we have learned from field research. In C. Seefeldt (Ed.), *Continuing issues in early childhood education* (pp. 245-60). Columbus, OH: Merrill.

Goffin, S. G. (1990). Government's responsibility in early childhood care and education: Reviewing the debate. In C. Seefeldt (Ed.), *Continuing issues in early childhood education* (pp. 9-23). Columbus, OH: Merrill.

Goodlad, J. I. (1986). *A place called school: Prospects for the future*. New York: McGraw-Hill.

Goodlad, J. I. (1988). Apples, diamonds, and glue. In G. F. Roberson & M. A. Johnson (Eds.), *Leaders in education* (pp. 45-57). Lanham, MD: University of America Press.

Gordon, I. J. (1977). Parent education and parent involvement: Retrospect and prospect. *Childhood Education*, 54, 71-79.

Gordon, I. J., & Breivogel, W. (Eds.). (1976). *Building effective home-school relationships*. Boston: Allyn & Bacon.

Gordon, I. J., Guinagh, B., & Jester, R. E. (1977). The Florida parent education infant and toddler programs. In M. C. Day & R. L. Parker (Eds.), *The preschool in action* (2nd ed.) (pp. 97-127). Boston: Allyn & Bacon.

Graham, P.A. (1976). America's unsystematic education system. In E.H. Grotberg (Ed.), *200 years of children* (pp. 134-147). Washington, DC: U. S. Government Printing Office.

Grant, W.V., & Eiden, L.J. (1982). *Digest of educational statistics*. Washington, DC: National Center for Educational Statistics.

Greven, P. (1977). *The Protestant temperament*. New York: Alfred A. Knopf.

Gross, R., & Gross, B. (1976). Lifelong learning. In E. H. Grotberg (Ed.), *200 years of children* (pp. 178-187). Washington, DC: U. S. Government Printing Office.

Grotberg, E. H. (1976). Child development. In E. H. Grotberg (Ed.), *200 years of children* (pp. 391-420). Washington, DC: U. S. Government Printing Office.

Grubb, W. N., & Lazerson, M. (1988). *Broken promises*. Chicago: University of Chicago Press.

Gulliford, A. (1984). *America's country schools*. Washington, DC: Preservation Press.

Gullo, F. (1990). The changing family context: Implications for the development of all-day kindergartens. *Young Children, 45* (4), 35-39.

Gunsberg, A. (1989). Empowering young abused and neglected children through play. *Childhood Education*, 66, 8-10.

Hall, G. S. (1883, May). The contents of children's minds. *The Princeton Review, 11*, 249-253.

Handlin, O. (1976). Education and the American society. In E. H. Grotberg (Ed.), *200 years of children* (pp. 125-133). Washington, DC: U. S. Government Printing Office.

Heath, K. G. (1976). The female equation. In E. H. Grotberg (Ed.), *200 years of children* (pp. 148-159). Washington, DC: U. S. Government Printing Office.

Henretta, J.A., Brownlee, W.E., Brody, D., & Ware, S. (1987). *American history since 1865*. Chicago: Dorsey Press.

Hewes, D. W. (1986). The kindergarten as an assimilation program for immigrants to the United States 1880 to 1900. In O. Vag (Ed.), *Historia infantie: International annual for the history of early childhood, Vol. III* (pp. 1-28). Budapest, Hungary: Eolvos Lorand University.

Hohmann, M., Banet, B., & Weikart, D. P. (1979). *Young children in action*. Ypsilanti: High/Scope Press.

Holmes Group (1986). *Tomorrow's teachers*. East Lansing, MI: Author.

Hopman, W. M. (1989). Interactional approaches to parent training. *Childhood Education*, 65, 167-168.

Honig, A.S. (1990). Infant/toddler education issues: Practices, problems, and promises. In C. Seefeldt (Ed.), *Continuing issues in early childhood education* (pp. 61-105). Columbus, OH: Merrill.

Honig, A., & Lally, R. (1981). *Infant caregiving: A design for training* (2nd ed.). Syracuse, NY: Syracuse University Press.

Hughes, F. (1991). *Children, play and development*. Boston: Allyn & Bacon.

Hunt, J. M. (1961). Intelligence and experience. New York: Ronald Press.

Hunter, R. (1965). The child. In *Poverty: Social conscience in the progressive era*. New York: Harper & Row (1965 edition of 1904 book).

Hymes, J.L. (1991). *Early childhood education: Twenty years in review*. Washington, DC: National Association for the Education of Young Children.

International Kindergarten Union (1924). A few facts about the International Kindergarten Union. Unpublished information release. ACEI Archives, Record Group 1, Box 1, History folder.

International Reading Association (1985). *Literacy development and pre-first grade*. Newark, DE: Author.

Johnson, J. E., Christie, J. F., & Yawkey, T. D. (1987). *Play and early childhood development*. Glenview, IL: Scott, Foresman.

Kaden, M. (1990). Issues on computers and early childhood education. In C. Seefeldt (Ed.), *Continuing issues in early childhood education* (pp. 264-272). Columbus, OH: Merrill.

Kadushin, A. (1974). *Child welfare services* (2nd ed.). New York: Macmillan.

Kamii, C. (1973). A sketch of the Piaget-derived preschool curriculum developed by the Ypsilanti early education program. In B. Spodek (Ed.), *Early childhood education (pp. 209-229)*. Englewood Cliffs, NJ: Prentice-Hall.

Kamii, C. (1985). Leading primary education toward excellence: Beyond worksheets and drill. *Young Children, 40* (6), 3-9.

Kantrowitz, B. (1991, June 10). Growing up under fire. *Newsweek*, 64.

Katz, L. G., & Chard, S. C. (1990). *Engaging children's minds*. Norwood, NJ: Ablex.

Keister, M. (1977). *The good life for infants and toddlers* (2nd ed.). Washington, DC: National Association for the Education of Young Children.

Keniston, K. (1975). Do Americans really like children? *Childhood Education, 52*, 4-12.

Keniston, K., & Carnegie Council on Children. (1977). *All our children: The American family under pressure*. New York: Harcourt Brace Jovanovich.

Klass, C. S., & Nall, S. W. (1989). Accessible professional development: A community-based program for early childhood educators. *Childhood Education, 65*, 224-227.

Krogh, S. (1990). *The integrated early childhood curriculum*. New York: McGraw-Hill.

Law, N.R. (1979) What is early childhood education? *Childhood Education, 55*, 200-204.

Lay-Dopyera, M., & Dopyera, J. (1990). The child-centered curriculum. In C. Seefeldt (Ed.), *Continuing issues in early childhood education* (pp. 207-222). Columbus, OH: Merrill.

Lawton, J.L. (1988). *Introduction to child care and early childhood education*. Glenview, IL: Scott, Foresman.

Lazar, I., & Darlington, R. (1982). Lasting effects of early education: A report from the Consortium for Longitudinal Studies. *Monograph of the Society for Research in Child Development*, Serial No. 195, *47* (2-3).

Leavitt, J.E. (1981). Helping abused and neglected children. *Childhood Education, 57*, 267-270.

Lundsteen, S. W., & Tarrow, N.B. (1981). *Guiding young children's learning*. New York: McGraw-Hill.

Manning, M., & Manning, G. (1981). The school's assault on childhood. In J. S. McKee, (Ed.), *Early childhood education 83/84* (pp. 174-177). Sluice Dock, CT: Dushkin Publishing Group.

McCarthy, M. A., & Houston, J. P. (1980). *Fundamentals of early childhood education*. Cambridge, MA: Winthrop.

Meisels, S. J. (1987). Uses and abuses of developmental screening and school readiness testing. *Young Children, 42*, (1), 4-6, 68-73.

Mindes, G. (1990). Kindergarten in our nation. In C. Seefeldt (Ed.), *Continuing issues in early childhood education* (pp. 107-120). Columbus, OH: Merrill.

Mitchell, A. (1989, May). Old baggage, new visions: Shaping policy for early childhood programs. *Phi Delta Kappan*, 655-672.

Montessori, M. (1967). *The absorbent mind* (Claude A. Claremont, Trans.). New York: Holt, Rinehart & Winston.

Morgan, G.G. (1983). Child day care policy in chaos. In E. F. Zigler, S. L. Kagan, & E. Klugman (Eds.), *Children, families, and government* (pp. 249-265). Cambridge, England: Cambridge University Press.

Morrison, G. (1988). *Early childhood education today* (4th ed.). Columbus, OH: Merrill.

National Association for the Education of Young Children (no date). *Accreditation by the National Academy of Early Childhood Programs*. Washington, DC: Author.

National Association of Early Childhood Specialists in State Departments of Education. (1987). *Unacceptable trends in kindergarten entry and placement*. Distributed by state departments of education.

National Commission on Excellence in Education. (1983). *A nation at risk: The imperative for educational reform*. Washington, DC: U. S. Government Printing Office.

National Institute of Education. (1985). *Becoming a nation of readers: The report of the Commission on Reading*. Washington, DC: Author.

Neugebauer, R. (1990, November/December). Child care's long and colorful past. *Child Care Information Exchange*, 5-9.

Nimnicht, G. (1973). Overview of responsive model program. In B. Spodek (Ed.), *Early childhood education* (pp. 199-208). Englewood Cliffs, NJ: Prentice-Hall.

Parker, S. C., & Temple, A. (1925). *Unified kindergarten and first-grade teaching*. Boston: Ginn & Co.

Patterson, K., & Wright, A. E. (1990). The speech, language or hearing-impaired child: At-risk academically. *Childhood Education, 67*, 91-95.

Perrone, V. (1991). On standardized testing. *Childhood Education, 67*, 132-142.

Perry, G. (1990). Alternate modes of teacher preparation. In C. Seefeldt (Ed.), *Continuing issues in early childhood education* (pp. 173-197). Columbus, OH: Merrill.

Piaget, J. (1963). *The origins of intelligence in children* (M. Cook, Trans.). New York: Norton.

Piscigallo, P. R. (1988, Fall). Preschool: Head Start or hard push? *Social Policy*, 45-48.

Postman, N. (1982). *The disappearance of childhood*. New York: Delacorte Press.

Prescott, E. (1974). Approaches to quality in early childhood programs. *Childhood Education, 50*, 125-131.

Public Health Service. (1976). 200 years of child health in America. In E. H. Grotberg (Ed.), *200 years of children* (pp. 61-122). Washington, DC: U. S. Government Printing Office.

Racial isolation in the public schools: A report of the U. S. Commission on Civil Rights. (1967). Washington, DC: U.S. Government Printing Office.

Ranck, E. R. (1990). There is no such thing as a free hunch: Following up on fortuitous events. Unpublished manuscript.

Reynolds, J. (1976). Two hundred years of children's recreation. In E. H. Grotberg (Ed.), *200 years of children* (pp. 285-321). Washington, DC: U. S. Government Printing Office.

Richardson, R. L. (1985). Wisdom-based junior high school teaching. *Childhood Education, 61*, 277-281.

Rousseau, J. J. (1933). *Emile* (B. Foxley, Trans.). London: J. M. Dent & Sons.

Schickedanz, J. A., Hansen, K., & Forsyth, P.D. (1990). *Understanding children*. Mountain View, CA: Mayfield.

Schorsch, A. (1979). *Images of childhood: An illustrated social history*. New York: Mayflower Books.

Shepard, L. A., & Smith, M. L. (1986). Synthesis of research on school readiness and kindergarten retention. *Educational Leadership, 48*, 78-86.

Shepard, L. A., & Smith, M. L. (1987). Effects of kindergarten retention at the end of first grade. *Psychology in the Schools, 24*, 346-357.

Shepard, L. A., & Smith, M. L. (1989). *Escalating kindergarten curriculum*. Urbana, IL: ERIC Clearinghouse on Elementary and Early Childhood Education.

Simmons, B., & Brewer, J. (1985). When parents of kindergartners ask "why?" *Childhood Education, 61*, 177-184.

Skeen, P., Robinson, B.E., & Flake-Hobson, C. (1984). Blended families: Overcoming the Cinderella myth. *Young Children, 39* (2), 64-74.

Skinner, B. F. (1953). *Science and human behavior.* New York: Macmillan.

Smith, I. L. (1942). *Half a century of progress 1892-1942.* Washington, DC: Association for Childhood Education.

Snapper, K. J. (1976). The American Legacy. In E. H. Grotberg (Ed.), *200 years of children* (pp. 13-38). Washington, DC: U. S. Government Printing Office.

Snyder, A. (1972). *Dauntless women in childhood education 1856-1931.* Washington, DC: Association for Childhood Education International.

Snyder, A. (1973). The roots of growth. *Childhood Education, 50,* 10-13.

Special report: The status of black children. (1989). *Black Child Advocate, 15* (4).

Spodek, B. (1973). *Early childhood education.* Englewood Cliffs, NJ: Prentice-Hall.

Spodek, B., Saracho, O., & Davis, M. (1991). *Foundations of early childhood education.* Englewood Cliffs, NJ: Prentice-Hall.

Stroman, S. H. & Duff, R. E. (1982). The latchkey child: Whose responsibility? *Childhood Education, 59,* 76-79.

Sudia, C. E. (1976). Historical trends in American family behavior: An essay. In E. H. Grotberg (Ed.), *200 years of children* (pp. 41-60). Washington, DC: U. S. Government Printing Office.

Tegano, D. W., Sawyers, J. K., & Moran, J. D. (1989). Problem-finding and solving in play: The teacher's role. *Childhood Education, 66,* 92-95.

Thorndike, E. L. (1910). *Educational psychology.* New York: Teachers College Press.

Thorndike, E. L. (1911). *Animal intelligence: Experimental studies.* New York: Macmillan.

U.S. Bureau of the Census (1980, July). *Characteristics of the population below the poverty level: 1978.* Washington, DC: U.S. Department of Health, Education, and Welfare.

Verzaro-Lawrence, M. (1980). Early childhood education: Issues for a new decade. *Childhood Education, 57,* 104-108.

Wallerstein, J. S. (1989, January 22). Children after divorce. *The New York Times Magazine,* 19-21, 41-44.

Weber, E. (1969). *The kindergarten: Its encounter with educational thought in America.* New York: Teachers College Press.

Weber, E. (1984). *Ideas influencing early childhood education.* New York: Teachers College Press.

Weiser, M. G. (1982). Public Policy: For or against children and families? An international perspective. *Childhood Education, 58,* 87-90.

Willis, A., & Riccuiti, H. *A good beginning for babies.* Washington, DC: National Association for the Education of Young Children.

Wingert, P., & Kantrowitz, B. (1990, Winter/Spring). The day care generation. *Newsweek* Special Issue, 86-87, 89, 92.

Wishon, P. M., & Spangler, R. S. (1990). The education of children in Japanese-American internment camps during WWII. Focus on kindergarten. Unpublished manuscript.

Wortham, S.C. (1985). Frontiers of challenge: Association for Childhood Education International 1985. *Childhood Education, 62,* 74-79.

Wortham, S. C., & Frost, J. L. (1990). *Playgrounds for young children: National survey and perspectives.* Reston, VA: American Alliance for Health, Physical Education, Recreation and Dance.

Zeir, C. (1933). Indian unit–Making Navajo bread. *Childhood Education, 10,* 80-82.

Zinmeister, K. (1990). Growing up scared. *The Atlantic, 265* (6), 49-66.

PHOTOGRAPH CREDITS

CHAPTER 1
Page 1-A Doll Named Alice. Alice and her wardrobe were listed in the ACEI Collection at the University of Maryland. Her wardrobe was located, but not Alice. She was later found in a glass cabinet at ACEI Headquarters. Photograph by Marshal Wortham.

Page 2-Girl on Chicago Street, circa 1900. Appeared on the cover of the January 1978 issue of *Childhood Education*. Photograph by Lewis Hine.

Page 2-Urban Playground, circa 1910. Source unknown.

Page 3-Urban Children, circa 1900-1920. Source unknown.

Page 4-"Their dear mother was not there." From *Alice and Her Mother* published by the American Sunday School Union in 1835. ACEI Collection, The University of Maryland.

Page 5-The Sisters. Frontspiece picture for *The Sisters* published by the American Sunday School Union in 1834. ACEI Collection, The University of Maryland.

Page 6-Mason Street School, San Diego, CA. Photograph by Marshal Wortham.

Page 7-The Old Country School, circa 1893. Photograph from Iowa State Historical Department.

Page 8-Froebel Yarn Balls. ACEI Collection, The University of Maryland. Photograph by Marshal Wortham.

CHAPTER 2
Page 11-Syrian Children at Mayer Chapel Kindergarten, 1910. From *Eliza A. Baker Her Life and Her Work* by Emma Law Thornburgh published by The Eliza A. Baker Club, Inc. and the Indiana Historical Society, 1956, p. 56a. ACEI Collection, University of Maryland.

Page 11-Childhood in California. Contributed by Marge Rasmussen

Page 12-Nested Egg Toy. ACEI Collection at ACEI Headquarters. Photograph by Marshal Wortham.

Page 13-Photograph of an Immigrant Family. *Childhood Education*, January 1977, p. 137. Photograph courtesy of Smithsonian Institution, Washington, D.C.

Page 15-Teacher. *Childhood Education*, May 1926, p. 440. Contributed to *CE* with accompanying poem by the Culver-Smith Training School, Hartford, CO.

Page 17-Block Building in the Kindergarten. 1932. ACEI Collection, The University of Maryland.

Page 17-Attucks Kindergarten, St. Louis. ACEI Collection, The University of Maryland.

Page 18-Boy Observing Chickens. ACEI Collection, The University of Maryland.

Page 21-Reception at Radcliffe to the Kindergarten Delegates. Appeared in the Boston Herald, April 24, 1902 with an article about the International Kindergarten Union Conference. ACEI Collection, The University of Maryland.

Page 21-Ruth Burritt. From an article written by Arnold Gesell, *Childhood Education*, January 1934, p. 172. Original is an engraving from the Historical Register, Centennial Exposition, Philadelphia, 1876.

Page 22-Photograph of the Delegates to the 1924 International Kindergarten Union Conference. ACEI Collection, The University of Maryland.

Page 22-Photograph of the Delegates to the 1932 Association of Childhood Education Annual Conference taken with President Herbert Hoover in Washington, D. C. ACEI Collection, The University of Maryland.

CHAPTER 3
Page 26-Boys Playing Baseball. *Childhood Education*, October 1950, p. 59. Photograph courtesy of Chicago Public Schools.

Page 26-Second Grade Boys Building an Airplane. *Childhood Education*, October 1933, p. 15. Photography by Central Park Studio, Battle Creek, MI.

Page 29-Preschool Children. *Childhood Education*, May 1940, p.390.

Page 30-Boy with a Violin. *Childhood Education*, February 1951, p. 267. Photograph courtesy of Margaret Hampel, Stillwater, Oklahoma.

Page 31-Unhurried, Joyous Living. *Childhood Education*, October 1933, p. 2. From "Singing As We Go." A book of Poetry Pieces for the Piano by George H. Gartlan and Elsie Jean. Illustrated by Mable Betsy Hill. Courtesy of Hinds, Hayden & Eldredge, Inc., Publisher.

Page 32-Children Working with Clay. ACEI Collection, University of Maryland.

Page 33-The Discipline of Makng Choices Begins Early. *Childhood Education*, March 1944, p. 294.

Page 35-Balloons. *Childhood Education*, March 1931, p. 338. From *Magpie Lane* by Nancy Byrd Turner. Illustrated by Decie Merwin. Courtesy of Harcourt, Brace & Company.

Page 36- Boy Peeping Through a Box. ACEI Collection, University of Maryland.

Page 38-Child in India Pictured with Educational Materials Sent by ACEI at the Request of the State Department after World War II. From 75 *Years of Concern For Children. History of the Association For Childhood Education.* by Winifred E. Bain, p. 23.

CHAPTER 4
Page 41-Girl with a Ball. Appeared on the cover of the May/June 1982 issue of *Childhood Education*. Photograph by Susie Fitzhugh, Baltimore, MD.

Page 42-Teacher and Child. Photographed in a classroom for migrant children,

1971. Photograph by Sue Wortham.

Page 43-Smiling Girl. *Childhood Education*, May 1973, p. 398. Photo courtesy of Teacher Corps, Washington, D. C.

Page 45-Urban Child. Appeared on the cover of the March 1974 issue of *Childhood Education*. Photograph by Arthur Tress, New York City.

Page 46-High School Vocational Students. *Childhood Education*, November/December, 1982, p. 83. Photograph by David S. Strickler, Newville, PA.

Page 48-Primary Grade Student in Class. Appeared on the cover of the November/December 1978 issue of *Childhood Education*. Photograph by Juliana Montfort, Chevy Chase, MD.

Page 49-Hispanic Children Painting. *Childhood Education*, February/March 1980, p. 211. Photograph courtesy of Modesto, CA, City Schools.

Page 50-Young Girl Coloring. ACEI Collection, The University of Maryland.

Page 51-Lakota Sioux Child and Elder. *Childhood Education*, November/December, 1982, p. 115. Photograph by Rita Means, Parmalee, SD.

Page 52-Toddlers on a Sliding Board. *Childhood Education*, January 1980, p. 130. Photograph by Donna J. Harris, Merrill-Palmer Institute.

Page 53-Photograph of Childhood Education Center Dedication Day, August 14, 1960. In *75 Years of Concerns For Children. History of the Association For Childhood Education International* by Winifred E. Bain, p. 46.

CHAPTER 5

Page 57-Preschool Friends. Appeared on the cover of theNovember/December 1985 issue of *Childhood Education*. Photograph by David M. Grossman, Brooklyn, NY.

Page 59-Disappearing Childhood. Appeared with an article by Neil Postman in *Childhood Education*, March/April 1985, p. 287. Photograph by Susan Batcheler, Indiana University of Pennsylvania.

Page 59-Inner City Children. *Childhood Education*, October 1972, p. 14. Photograph by Arthur Tress from an exhibit portfolio, *Open Spaces in the Inner City*, produced by the New York Council on the Arts.

Page 60-Teenages of the 1980s. *Childhood Education*, March/April 1985. Photograph by Susie Fitzhugh, Baltimore, MD.

Page 61-Outdoor Play. Appeared on the cover of the November/December 1983 theme issue of *Childhood Education* titled, "The New Arrivals." Photograph by Juan Tituana, Center for Young Chidlren, University of Maryland.

Page 62-Young Child of the 1970s. Appeared on the cover of the October 1975 theme issue of *Childhood Education* titled, "Valuing the Dignity of Children." Photograph by Susie Fitzhugh, Baltimore, MD.

Page 63-Girl with Blocks. *Childhood Education*, November/December 1983, p. 97. Photograph by Guillermina Engelbrecht.

Page 64-Boy in a Tree. Appeared on the October 1978 cover of *Childhood Education*. Photograph by Jim Cohen, Washington, DC.

Page 65-Male Adolescent. Appeared on the March/April 1984 theme issue of *Childhood Education* titled "Teaching for Thinking." Photograph by Ron Meyer, White Eyes Design, Fresno, OH.

Page 67-Two Early Adolescents. Appeared on the March/April 1985 theme issue of *Childhood Education* titled, "Adolescents: Their Needs and Concerns." Photograph by Jim Cronk, Photographic Illustrations, Mr. Lebanon, PA.

Page 69-Preschool Children. *Childhood Education*, October 1978, p. 23. Photograph by Juliana Montfort, Chevy Chase, MD.

Page 69-Teacher and Children. *Childhood Education*, October 1975, p. 18. Photograph by Susie Fitzhigh, Baltimore, MD.

Page 74-Early Froebelian Kindergarten. ACEI Collection, ACEI Headquarters.

Page 75-Some Former Presidents of IKU and ACE Photographed at the 1936 ACE Conference in New York City. Front row, l. to r.: Caroline Barbour 1927-29, Edna Dean Baker 1933-35, Lucy Wheelock 1894-99, Stella Louise Wood 1917-18, Patty Smith Hill 1908-09. Back row: Julia Wade Abbott 1931-33, Alice Temple 1925-27, Margaret Holmes 1929-31, Catherine Watkins 1915-17, Ella Ruth Boyce, 1923-25. Appeared in *Childhood Education*, November/December 1985, p. 75. ACEI Collection.